# YOUNG MAN ARISE!
## *Fresh Hope Emerging from the Darkness*

BY

BRIAN V. WARTH

*Lead Pastor, Chapel of Change Christian Fellowship*
*Long Beach, California*

# ENDORSEMENTS

*"The story of Brian Warth and **Young Man Arise!** will stir your soul and give you a crystal clear picture of the AMAZING power of God's redemptive grace. If you have ever felt that God could never use a person like you, then you need to read this book. It will destroy any negative thought you may have about getting a second chance on life."*
Dudley Rutherford, Lead Pastor
Shepherd of the Hills Church, Los Angeles
Author, ***God Has an App for That***

*"Great ministers of Christ usually possess both in-depth knowledge of Him and personal experience with character forming trials. **Young Man Arise!** is a destiny altering look into the life of a man who harnesses both. Pastor Brian Warth has a unique message of redemption produced not only from study on the subject but acquaintance with its reality."*
Wayne Chaney, Lead Pastor
Antioch Church, Long Beach
Visionary, Long Beach Gospel Fest

# TABLE OF CONTENTS

# SPECIAL THANKS TO:

Kristy Hinds for becoming one with my story
and helping me express it through the written word.

# DEDICATION:

This book is dedicated to the memory of my oldest brother
who did not survive the streets.
David Ralph Aldrete, II
September 11, 1966 – January 14, 1982

# PREFACE:

This is a true story but a hard one to tell. The names of some people have been changed to prevent any more hurt. And I confess from the start that I tell it from my perspective and memory. I was compelled to write my story for the greater good. The world is so wrecked with hopelessness and despair that every now and then there needs to be a story of redemption and restoration that emerges from the darkness, to infuse fresh hope in the hearts of people. By God's grace, this is one.

"Now it happened, the day after, that He went into a city called Nain; and many of His disciples went with Him, and a large crowd. And when He came near the gate of the city, behold, a dead man was being carried out, the only son of his mother; and she was a widow. And a large crowd from the city was with her. When the Lord saw her, He had compassion on her and said to her, 'Do not weep.' Then He came and touched the open coffin, and those who carried him stood still. And He said, 'Young man, I say to you, arise.' So he who was dead sat up and began to speak. And He presented him to his mother" (Luke 7: 11-15, NKJV).

## CHAPTER 1

# BACK IN THE DAYS

For a gang member in Los Angeles in the '80s, every day was the weekend. Life seemed like one big party filled with beer bottles, shot glasses, and waves of heavy smoke. My brothers and sister were older than me and had more freedom to do what they wanted. I would try to stay up late with them, but gang life was the last thing my mom wanted for me. It was a hard knock life for a seven-year-old boy, when everyone else in the house could stay up late to do whatever he or she pleased. On Thursday nights, my mom usually gave me a break because the good TV detective shows came on like "Magnum P.I." and "Hawaii 5-0." Most people watched those shows and rooted for the cop. I sometimes had a soft spot for the bad guys, probably because they resembled some of the people that came through my house.

"Brian, don't sit so close to the TV, *beijo!*" my mom said with grief.

This was not the first time we were having this conversation. I did not move. I was not paying attention.

"Brian, watch the TV from the couch or scoot back a little!"

"I'm not even that close, Mom!"

"Scoot, back. I'm not going to say it again. You'll get bad eye-sight sitting that close."

Grudgingly, I finally scooted back a few inches.

Our house was in the middle of the barrio, a term for a Hispanic-dominated neighborhood. My mom and dad never married and I have no memories of them ever together. My brothers, sister, and I lived with my mom and her boyfriend. I had a different dad than the rest of my family. I got to spend time with my dad on the weekends sometimes. But this was my mom's weekend. I could hear voices coming from the kitchen. I looked over my shoulder and saw my mom arguing with my oldest brother, David.

"All right, I'm leaving and I'll be back later."

"Where are you going?"

"Just out to kick it with some of my friends. I'll be back."

"David, it's the same thing every weekend. Can't you stay home tonight?"

"Naw, Mom I got plans."

"Why don't you at least stay to have some spaghetti?"

"I'm not hungry."

"What do you mean, you're not hungry? I don't want you out there drinking or getting high, David. You're only fifteen years old."

"Mom, I don't have time for this. I'll see you later."

"Don't be too late! I need you to watch Brian for me a little bit."

"Yeah, all right, Mom. Maybe."

I heard the door slam.

"Love you." My mom's words trailed off before David could hear her.

Frustrated, my mom walked around the kitchen, kind of talking under her breath. I just wanted everyone to be quiet and respect my show time. Lately, my mom and David argued more often about him coming and going all of the time. Upset, I guess my mom decided to go out instead of making the spaghetti.

"Brian, I'm going to the mall with your sister. I'll be back in a little while."

"All right."

"Peter and Larry are here."

"Okay, cool."

I went back to watching television.

Peter was my older brother too, but he was younger than David. Larry was my mom's current boyfriend and he lived at the house with us. I don't know what time it was, but I do know at least two hours of my shows had ended before I heard the doorbell ring. I was not allowed to answer the door by myself, since I was only seven. However, since my mom was not home, I raced for the door and swung it open without looking through the peephole, because I was still too short to reach.

A tall kid dressed in all black stood at the door. He was sporting a black Raiders t-shirt and black pants we called Dickeys. I remember he had on a pair of those black-and-white All-Star Converse sneakers. My brother David had a pair and my mom did not like them. I stared up at the kid at the door. I recognized him from our barrio. I did not know his name, but I knew he was one of David's homeboys. We referred to our friends as homeboys. He just looked down at me kind of nervously while shaking his head.

"You're David's little brother, right?"

I just kept looking at him.

"Your brother is David? Right?"

I shook my head up and down in affirmation.

"Your brother's been shot dead up the street. Go tell your mom, but don't tell her I told you."

Within seconds, he was gone.

I just stood there for a moment. I heard what he said, but it did not register. I could not understand what was happening. David was just here in the kitchen a little while ago. Why was this guy saying that he was dead? Suddenly, just as I had time to imagine the grim scene of my brother lying bloodied on a street corner, I could feel fear creeping up my body to a boiling point of panic. Finally, I was able to move from that cemented place at the door. I turned to run and tell Peter and Larry, but they were already at the door, questioning me about who had been there. Peter demanded to know why I looked so scared. I could hear the faint sounds of sirens in the background. Sirens were not an uncommon sound in my barrio. However, I knew these were for my brother.

I swallowed the lump in my throat and said, "David's been shot. He got shot up the street."

In that moment, Peter and Larry reminded me of Fred and Barney Rubble from the Flintstones. Whenever Fred and Barney were trying to leave the house in a hurry, they moved their feet really fast but it would take a second for them to actually move and get going. It felt like everything was in slow motion, but I knew we were all moving as fast as we could. Peter made me swear not to open the door until they came back.

"And no matter what, do not tell Mom about David!"

After a while, Peter and Larry came back to the house. Both of them looked distraught, but no one said anything to me. I started to think maybe David was okay. Larry reminded me again not to say anything to my mom until he had a chance to talk to her. No sooner than I had promised not to say anything, I heard my mom's car pull up into the driveway. I looked out the window and saw she was home. Just as my mom was getting out of the car, I darted past everyone in the house and ran out of the door.

"Mom! Mom! David got shot! David got shot!" I yelled.

I just thought I wanted to be the one to tell her. I knew my mom would know what to do. I thought if I told my mom right away, then we could find out what was going on with David.

It was not long before everyone was outside. Family and friends had already begun to gather at the house. They all came outside to greet my mom and me. Some of my family glared at me with mean looks because I told my mom about David. I did not care. I felt like it was my job to be the one to tell her. Soon, I felt hands on my shoulders, guiding me away from my mother, ushering me back into the house. Peter yelled at me to go inside. Quickly, I glanced back and saw my mom running back to her car and fumbling with the keys. I assumed she was going to go pick up David from wherever he was at.

My mom found David.

My brother lay dead in the county hospital, executed by a single gunshot wound to his face, delivered by the hands of one of his own homeboys. My mom did not make it to the hospital on time to hold her son, show him comfort, or hold his hand for his last moments. The last thing she had said to him was to stay home for spaghetti. My oldest brother died on a Thursday night. I never had the chance to say goodbye.

Weeks and even months after David's funeral, it was hard to be in the house without thinking about him. My mom allowed David's room to be set up like a shrine. Except this was not a golden palace dedicated to a fallen hero or leader. David's shrine resembled the inner patchwork of my barrio's lifestyle. All of the walls in his room were covered in a mosaic of graffiti rituals and symbolism.

Someone wrote a gangster's poem in David's memory:

*To: Casper*
*I have a story to tell you about one Chicano, yeah.*
*He wore the khakis and sometimes a derby too,*
*but that was the part of him seen by all of you.*
*He would come home late, or wouldn't come home at all.*
*His hair was combed back and he was sort of tall.*
*I never could count the girls that use to call.*
*He was very bright and funny and Casper was his name.*
*But he's gone now. They've taken him away.*
*Not to prison but somewhere farther away.*
*You see somebody shot him down.*
*His homeboys broken hearted as he laid on the ground.*
*I love you, Casper, and I know you are in Heaven.*
*I pray to God all is forgiven.*
*Love Always,*
*Your Homeboy,*
*-Goofy*

David's face was drawn as a silhouette on the wall. A hole was carved out where the bullet entered his face. This was the art, heart, and memory of a young gangster's life. Initially, I found it hard to walk into his room because it was just a reminder that he was not coming back. In time I got used to the fact that David was gone.

One afternoon I was home alone, hoping someone would come back to be with me. I did not feel safe at our house. I was lonely and a little scared, so I walked into David's room to pass the time. I slowly pushed the door open and stepped inside of the darkness. The curtains were closed and the room smelled of dust and dry air.

Everything was still the way David had left it, as if he would come back at any moment. I looked up at the walls, staring at all of the added graffiti that some of David's homeboys had drawn in grief. Finally, my eyes wandered over to the silhouette drawn of him on the wall. I could not hold back and broke down in tears. I missed my big brother, and someone had shot him dead. I ran up to the wall and began to punch the silhouette. I was angry and could not understand why he was gone. Soon, I grew tired of fighting and slowly walked out of the room. I pulled the door closed without turning back for a last look. I rarely went into David's room after that day.

Being left alone had become the standard at my house. David's presence and the heaviness of the tragedy were still heavy on everyone's mind. My mom hardly stayed home anymore. Sometimes she would leave for hours, and when she came home I could tell she had been drinking. My brothers and sisters would also leave the house to party. Often I was left alone, just waiting for someone to come back. Since David's death, I was scared to be alone, thinking someone would come to shoot at the house.

I also remember watching the news and hearing about a man named Richard Ramirez, who was going around sneaking into houses and killing people. The news called him the Night-Stalker. I saw a lady on the television crying. I thought I overheard her say that she came home and found her daughter was stabbed and the Night-Stalker was the reason. Now, I had to worry about being shot and a Night-Stalker breaking into the house and stabbing me. I could not handle the fear. I was only ten years old and did not want to die. I began coming up with unique plans to keep myself safe. Sometimes I would ride my bike up and down the street until someone came home. One night, late in the evening, I got tired of riding and people started saying I needed to go back into my house. I do not know how many times I had pedaled up and down that block, avoiding going into the house alone out of fear.

Eventually, I went back home. I walked into the house and turned on all the lights. I did not want to be in the dark. I would not even go to the bathroom, because I heard on the news that the Night-Stalker would come through the bathroom window. Instead, I went to sleep underneath my bed with a hammer in one hand and a cap gun in the other.

Things in my house never seemed to get better after David died. My mom was going out to drink more and more. I think this was to avoid the memories at home. I would cry whenever she left, sometimes chase her up the street in tears, but I think she was just too sad to stay around. My older brothers and sisters were hanging out with their friends more than ever before. I had a different father than the rest of my siblings. Recently, my brothers' and sister's dad had been sentenced to life in prison for murder. My mom would take us to visit him in Folsom Prison. The news of this traveled quickly to my father, and he immediately stopped her from taking me there ever again.

My dad acted like a drill sergeant at home, and being at his house was like being in the military compared to my mom's place. My dad was born on the Island of Guam and moved to the United States as a young man. Being the oldest of five children made my dad strong and protective. Not long after arriving in the States, my dad joined the U.S. Army and fought in the Vietnam War at age nineteen. By the time I was born, my father was a disabled veteran, and had fathered two children from a previous relationship. I am not exactly sure what led my father to be so strict and rigid. Perhaps it was the violence and terror of war and the things he saw that made him different. However, my dad was not the kind of man to complain or talk about his emotions, especially in the presence of his kids. He was just the way he was, and as his kid I had to accept this fact.

After David's death, tension started growing more and more between my mom and dad. They were both so different. My mom grew up in a Mexican-cultured environment. Her life was woven into the lifestyle our barrio represented. My mom had a lot of half-brothers and sisters. She was a lot more open about her past than my dad was about his. But when David died, her heart was broken, and I think going out to bars helped her to forget for a few moments the torture of having a son who had been murdered.

With my brothers' father in prison and David murdered, my father wanted me to live with him now more than ever. Of course, my mom did not want me to go. Therefore, the long, bitter custody battle for my future began with an ugly fight. My parents would stoop to low tactics to find a way to undermine one another. I remember my dad taking photos once of my mom's dirty house to use to prove neglect. I started learning big court words after spending hours in hearings in the family law courts. The judge would ask me who I wanted to live with, but my answer was always the same, "I don't know." I spent most of my childhood being shuttled back and forth between my mom's and dad's houses.

By the time I was eleven years old, my remaining brothers and sisters were all gang members. Our environment revolved around gang culture. This became our way of life and all we knew. On most days, my siblings' homeboys would hang out at our house. We called sitting around, hanging out at people's houses a kickback. The homeboys and homegirls would come over for the kickback and I would sit around, watching everyone get drunk and high. I used to like those nights because I was not alone; plus, I received a lot of attention. When I was hungry, the gang members would cook food for me or give me money to buy candy. I looked forward to spending time with everybody from the barrio. I started imagining what it would be like when I was old enough to hang out in the streets of the barrio and be just like them.

Tragedy was never far from my family. One afternoon, my brother Peter had to go to the courthouse in the City of Compton to clear up a traffic ticket, but he did not have a ride home, so he took the bus. While he was walking to the bus station, several gang members pulled up along side of Peter and began shooting at him. Peter was only eighteen years old when his body was riddled with bullets at close range. But he would live to see another day.

My mom thought having two brothers shot and one deceased would have deterred me from wanting to join a gang. However, life would soon lead me down the same path. Gang life would be my reality by the time I hit junior high school.

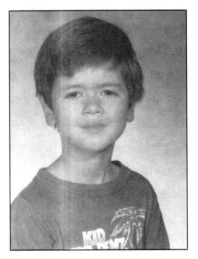

Brian, about age 7

David before joining a gang

David after joining a gang

David's funeral;

Brian is seated toward left side

## CHAPTER 2

# GIRLS, GANGS, AND GUNS

I n the fall of 1987, I turned twelve just before Halloween. Because of all the violence in my barrio, my mom decided to move us across town. However, at this point, moving out of the barrio was pointless. I usually rode my bike back to the barrio where my friends still lived. I would stay out late on the streets past midnight or even one o'clock in the morning.

I was not officially in a gang, but most of my friends and family were gang members. In my barrio, you cannot keep hanging around with gang members and not become an official member.

I loved being around the older kids in the gang. I admired them and felt safe with them. For Halloween, I decided to borrow David's shirt and black sunglasses. We had a costume day at school and my costume idea was to dress as a cholo. In the barrio, the term cholo referred to a Mexican male who wore baggy pants, oversized shirts, and was deemed a troublemaker.

I thought it was funny, dressing as a cholo for Halloween. I was too naïve at the time to realize that I was making a very big statement. While other kids were dressed in superhero costumes or as his or her favorite celebrity, I chose to wear a black jersey and baseball hat that represented my gangster heroes. Wearing that costume to school made me feel tough and proud. But as it turned out, the costume was not the best idea. Wearing David's clothes marked me as a gang member by some of the kids at school. My initiation into a gang would only be a matter of time.

The average kids my age were thinking about getting together on the weekend to hit up the movies to see *Beverly Hills Cop II*. I, on the other hand, was checking to see what my friends in the barrio had planned. I did not go out seeking gang life, but everyone I knew was in a gang or hanging out with a gang. At this point in my life, school seemed pointless. I would stay out late and my mom stopped saying anything to me about coming home early. As long as I was with the homeboys from the barrio, I felt like I was untouchable and everything was good.

One night before school, without much thought, I decided to shave my head. In my neighborhood, shaved heads were synonymous with gang bangers. The next day after shaving my head, I went to school feeling cool. I even started having a little clout with the ladies, even though I was tall and skinny back then. Lately, my demeanor had been changing. I felt my confidence building the more I hung out with the homeboys in the barrio.

One day in English class, while my teacher stepped out of the room, I started teasing a girl a few seats in front of me. I caught her checking me out with my new haircut. I was a jokester and found that teasing girls was an easy way to flirt. Even though I technically was not in a gang yet, I felt like I had some of the rights and privileges because of my affiliation with them. Ever since costume day and the change in my attitude, I noticed some of the guys in my class seemed to treat me differently. Shaving my head only increased the tension. While talking to the girl in my class, I caught this fool mad dogging me from across the room. I glanced at him a few times, not wanting any trouble, but I knew I could not back down. This kid was bigger than me, and so I glanced at the door, hoping our English teacher would come back soon. But he did not.

"Fool, what's your problem?" said the guy.

"What's your problem? I didn't even say nothing to you," I responded.

"You know that's my homeboy's girl, right?"

"I'm not even trying to get at her. Don't trip!"

"Fool, don't tell me not to trip!"

"Whatever, that's on you."

The conversation started to become more intense, and everyone in the classroom started egging us on with laughter and phrases like, "Awww, you going to take that?" The instigation from the rest of the students left both of us without room to walk away from this situation. I really started hoping the teacher would come back. When the guy got out of his seat and started crossing the classroom toward me, I wished I had never talked to this girl. She was not that cute anyway. But I could not back down now.

Just a few feet away, I looked at the guy, threw my arms out to the side with my palms facing up, and said, "So what's up?" This gesture basically welcomed a fight. However, I was surprised when the kid said, "I would mess you up right now, but I know your gang will get me." I sat in shock, unable to respond as he backed away, and then the teacher returned. I could not believe it. He thought I was in a gang. I was not in a gang yet, but maybe things would have to change. I was glad the argument was over. I felt a sense of honor in that moment, proud to be associated with gang members. I suddenly understood the power that gang members felt. I wanted to feel that confident and protected every day.

After that episode at school, I started hanging out with the homeboys more and more. I would ditch school and go to afternoon kickbacks at the park or someone's house. I had even been pulled over while walking and questioned by the police about my gang affiliation. I felt powerful and in control. I was no longer just tall and skinny Brian who had been David's little brother. I was becoming my own man. Unfortunately, I did not realize the price I would inevitably pay to join this gang.

It was a sunny day and I was supposed to be in school. Instead, a bunch of friends and I went cruising around the city looking for some fun to get into. There were about six of us in the bed of a gold, lowered mini truck, with my friend Carlos behind the wheel. Mini trucks were a hit back then – small pick-up trucks, usually Nissans or Toyotas that people decked up with small, fat tires and shiny rims. If it was really hooked up, the bed would have hydraulics on it to lift it up and down. At the very least it was slammed low to the ground.

As we pulled into a park in our barrio, one of my friends pulled out a fat joint of weed, and lit it up. He started to pass it around so that everyone could get a chance to take a hit. Puff, pass, puff, pass was the unwritten rule. If you stayed with the joint too long, you would be labeled as a bogard.

I was about the third in line and my heart started to beat faster as I watched the joint move around the circle. This was not the first time that I had been around people smoking weed. I remember as a little kid busting into my brother's smoked-filled room. But I had never smoked it before. I just chose not to.

When the joint got to me, I denied it as usual. "I don't smoke weed," I said. And that was true. I must have told my friends "no" a thousand times. I watched as the joint slowly made its way around the circle. My defenses lowered every time it was passed to a new hand. "Why do I keep saying no?" I thought. "I may as well try it, at least just once. One time is not going to kill me."

When the joint came back around to me, I did not wait for someone to ask again. To everyone's surprise, I grabbed it between my thumb and first finger, put it to my lips, and inhaled deeply, as if I knew what I was doing. I took a big hit. Immediately, I coughed the smoke out several times. I felt numb, as if I were losing control of my senses. My eyes started to burn. Then I got really paranoid. I thought my mom was going to walk up any time, yank the shell window open, and bust me.

My real problem though, was that it was not "just one time," as I had intended. Instead, I started smoking weed every chance I got. That really messed up my attitude even more.

I knew my day to get jumped-in was coming. We called gang initiation being "jumped-in". Being jumped-in is like a rite-of-passage. In my gang, there were three occasions when after a time agreed on by other members, a new member could be initiated. The initiation was a triple set of beatings that took place unexpectedly during a regular kickback. Sometimes someone would get stomped out really bad. I never understood why your own homeboys would try hard to hurt you.

As teenagers, there were not too many places we could go late at night. Not to mention we had a group of minors and young adults drinking, smoking pot, and experimenting with newer, harder drugs like cocaine and PCP. Many nights we headed to the beach to just hang out and joke around. I would follow the group, not wanting to be left behind at home. Peter sometimes made a scene, asking me why I was there and saying that I needed to leave. I was not interested in listening to anything he had to say. How could he tell me not to hang out, when he was the first one in line to party? All that was on my mind was becoming officially from our barrio's gang. I would soon get my wish.

It was a winter night, but the air felt warm for some reason. This was one of those nights that everyone was a little antsy and did not have anywhere to be. Someone made the suggestion and shouted, "Hey, let's go kick it at the beach. Who's down?" I was never one to turn down an opportunity to be in the mix. I was one of the first to hop into one of the low rider cars, and we headed down to the beach.

The beach was a regular spot for us at night. The strip of sand near the ocean was void of lights. We could be rowdy and out of control without anyone interfering. On occasion the cops would come out to comb the beach for partiers, but we would see them coming and scatter. Tonight, I knew the cops would be the least of my worries. I had a feeling that tonight was the night I would earn my stripes and be jumped-in. The fact that I was David and Peter's little brother could not hold my weight in the barrio any longer. The time had come for me to be an official member.

There was a big group of us out there that night. Midget, Kiki, Wacky, just to name a few. We were standing in clusters, folks just talking, joking, and drinking mostly. I noticed a group was forming off to my right, and voices were kind of hushed. I swallowed hard and tried not to be nervous, but I could feel a fluttering in my stomach. Who was I kidding? I was nervous, but ready. Suddenly, someone hit me from the side across the head. The blow was stacked with blunt force. Caught off guard, I fell to the ground quickly. At twelve, I was already almost six feet tall, but I barely weighed any-thing. I hit the ground like a bag of sand. I could not tell who was punching or kicking, but the blows were coming fast, hard, and from every direction. The beating was only moments, but it felt like I was scrunched there for half an hour.

Just as quickly as the poundings had come, the punches and kicks began to ease up. Slowly, I sat up, hoping I was still in one piece. Suddenly, the same hands that beat me down were reaching out to help me up and pat me on the back. I had done it. I was officially from the gang. Apart from the pain from the barrage of punches and kicks, everything inside of me was on fire that night. I felt like I was flying. I was filled with an enormous sense of pride. I finally belonged.

By the summer of 1989, I was thirteen and had already been officially in my gang for a year. It felt good not to "just" kick it with the group anymore. Now, I had earned my place as one of the homeboys. I was still David's little brother, but I was beginning to have my own level of respect. Instead of the gang just being my brothers' homeboys, they were mine too. Now, I was one of them.

The summer was always a party time, I guess because there was no school. We spent most of the time on the streets, doing a bunch of nothing. One of the homeboys had a car and every day was basically the same schedule. We would stay out late, cruising around until the early hours of the morning. We would end up sleeping until the afternoon the following day and just start the routine all over again.

I remember one day being especially hot. I woke up in the afternoon after a late night of partying. I paged one of my friends on his beeper and got dressed, waiting for him to pick me up. My mom was at work and I knew I would not see her. I got up and looked in the fridge for something to eat. But before I knew it, my homeboy had rolled up to the house and was waiting for me outside. I could hear the base from his ten-inch Woofer speakers rattling the front windows. I grabbed my black jacket because I knew I would still be out late into the night. Living in the Harbor area of Los Angeles made us close to the ocean. It could be really hot in the day, but then windy and cold at night. I threw on my black and white Nike Cortez shoes and hit the streets, eager for the day's adventure. My friend still had the car running. I hopped into the back and it was four of us in the car.

"What's up, homie?" I said to the driver.

"What up. What took you so long?" he replied.

"I just got up."

"Yeah, I feel you."

I noticed that N.W.A tape on the dashboard.

"When did you get that?" I pointed at the music tape.

"Aaaaaaa, you got to hear this song. We were bumpin' it when we pulled up."

"Rewind it and let me hear it."

After a short intro, I started to hear the beat drop. I was bobbing my head to the music and we were all feeling the lyrics to the chorus.

*"Gangsta, gangsta, that's what they're yellin'*
*It's not about a salary, it's about reality/ Gangsta, gangsta."*
[N.W.A, Gangsta Gangsta, Straight Outta Compton, 1988.]

The sounds of N.W.A shook the car and rattled the windows as we cruised down the street.

"Let me borrow this!" I said to the driver.

"I just got it."

I leaned back in my seat and enjoyed the ride. Before long, I saw my friend looking in the rearview mirror.

"Damn, the police are behind us."

"I'm tired of these fools," said my homeboy in the passenger seat as he glanced in the side mirror.

We were prepared to be pulled over by the cops and go through the whole routine, which consisted of a search for drugs, and then just harassing us and asking us what we were doing. This game of cat and mouse was part of our day, and kind of expected. We were smart enough never to have anything out in the open that we could get in trouble for. Just as everybody started checking their pockets, the cops turned on their sirens and swooped around past us, but not without first staring into the car. It looked like we got saved from going through the drama. Obviously they got called to go and handle some crime. Sirens and violence were the standard norm going into the 1990s.

After the police sped away, everybody relaxed a little bit. We shared a couple of expletives about the police, how they had nothing better to do, then we kept listening to the music. I remember the lyrics said:

*"Homies all standin' around, just hangin'*
*Some dope dealin', some gang bangin'*
*We decide to roll and we deep."*
[N.W.A, Gangsta Gangsta, Straight Outta Compton, 1988.]

The lyrics were written as if the rappers had taken a page from our lives.

Just as I was drifting off into my own thoughts, I felt the car start to slow down. I leaned up to see why we were slowing down and saw the answer right away. Four girls were walking down the street. We pulled up alongside of them. We did not know them, but I did recognize one of the girls. I think she lived in a neighborhood nearby that was separated from us by an Alpha Beta grocery store.

My two homeboys in the front seat immediately started talking to the girls from the car window as our car continued to slow down. At first they tried to ignore us, but that did not last long. One of the girls, I think she was the oldest one, came up to the car and asked what we were up to. Soon all of my homeboys were exchanging numbers. There was one girl who kind of hung back from the others. I saw her glancing at me in the back seat from the sidewalk. I sat back a little further in my seat, peering at her from underneath the brim of my Raiders hat.

The driver of the car was known for being outspoken. He said to the girl who appeared to be the ladies' spokesperson, "What's up with your friend back there? She doesn't feel like talking?"

"That's my god-sister. She's cool. She's just kind of quiet."

"Oh, yeah? My homeboy in the backseat likes quiet girls."

"Well, why doesn't he ask her for her number?" she said, pointing at me, but still looking at my friend.

I felt kind of awkward, but I did not have to worry for long. Soon the girls got tired of messing with us and decided to walk away. I knew I had seen the quiet girl around the barrio. She was cute. She was short and her hair was curly and styled like a lot of girls in the barrio, but something was different about her. Since her friends had traded numbers with my homeboys, I knew I would see her again. The barrio was not that big, and inevitably I would probably run into her at a party. As we started to drive off, I glanced out the window and I saw the quiet girl was still looking at me. My homeboy in the backseat noticed me looking at her.

"I think her name is Laura," he said quietly.

I was right. I did see Laura around at some of the kickbacks over the summer. We were thirteen when we met. Although I felt confident by being in the gang, I was still a little nervous about stepping to a chick, also known as asking a girl for her number. I was too focused on having fun. I did finally end up with her number and we talked on the phone every now and then, and that was cool.

The fun would soon turn into pain.

Brian, age 13

Brian, age 15

## CHAPTER 3

# SHOTS FIRED

I turned fourteen in October of 1989. I felt like fourteen was a milestone. I was in the same gang that David had been in, and I was only one year younger than he was when he died. I was fourteen and still alive. I started to feel haunted as days passed. Just knowing that David died near my age and in the same gang left me feeling unsettled and paranoid.

My dad was increasingly on me about my bad attitude. He was determined to see me not end up like my brother David or many of the other gang members in my barrio.

Gang life had exploded in Los Angeles. The news would tell about the rise of exceptionally violent gangs. I remember hearing about one gang member being kidnapped and tortured in a dark park. My dad continued to warn me that I would have no future if I stayed hanging around gang members, but I never listened. I ignored him.

I spent a weekend over at my dad's place because he wanted to celebrate my birthday with me. I was only with my dad for a few hours before I became antsy, ready to return to the barrio. My dad had too many rules at his house. I was becoming more withdrawn and rebellious.

My mom sent my brother Peter to drive over and pick me up. I stepped out of the house, glad to see my brother's low rider car. Back then the gangster cars where Buick Regals and Chevy Monte Carlos with little tires and shiny rims with spokes. I knew we would be bumping loud music and hitting the streets of the barrio as soon as we rolled out.

That day, my dad seemed even more upset than usual about my attitude. Also, my dad had a big problem with my brother Peter. He hated Peter's lifestyle. He felt there was no mistaking Peter's involvement in gangs, and if I continued to hang out with him that my life would be cut short. Before I could even make it out the driveway to the car, my father rushed past me and blocked me from getting in. No one on my mom's side of the family got along with my dad. My father was aggressive and had no problem speaking his mind. Peter got out of the car, and I knew there would be trouble. I stepped in between their argument and told my dad that I was leaving with my brother. But my dad wouldn't budge, so Peter left me behind. This really got me mad.

A few days later, I finally made it out to my barrio. Feeling bored and with nothing to do, I thought about spray-painting in my rival gang's barrio. Lately, I had taken to spray-painting. I felt like spraying on the walls of those fools' barrio was a non-violent way of staying active in the gang war. I got pretty good at getting in and out of the rival gang's barrio without being noticed. However, lately I had been chased out and shot at, but I was fast and no one caught me. Spray-painting gave me an adrenaline rush. You had to be bold to walk into your rival gang's barrio in bright daylight and write on their walls. I felt like I was contributing to our battle; however, a battle that I had not started and certainly would not finish.

I went with my gut. I still could not shake that paranoid feeling that I had about turning fifteen, so I changed my mind about spray-painting and headed over to Peter's apartment. Peter lived off of Main Street. This area was like a neutral territory that separated us from our rival gang, but it was still dangerous if you got caught by yourself.

I heard about a football game going on that day at the park. Local gangs had developed a tradition of playing football against gangs from outside of our own area of Los Angeles. My gang was playing against a gang from the west side of Los Angeles. I showed up at Peter's, but he was not home. His girlfriend let me into the apartment and I played with my seven-year-old niece for a little bit. Finally, I got bored and decided to head out.

"Hey, Bianca, I'm leaving. Come lock the door," I said.

"Where you going?"

"Up to the park to watch the football game. Just tell Peter I went up there."

"All right, I don't know when he's coming back."

"Yeah, all right, well, just tell him where I went," I said as I exited the apartment, onto the street.

My brother's apartment building reminded me of an old-style hotel. Something you would see in the movies from the 1960s. From Peter's apartment, I could see Main Street, but we were protected, so I thought, by a cinderblock eight-foot wall that stood ten feet away from the front door. I could hear traffic from the freeway up ahead. I was wearing a brand new black jersey. I had just recently got new clothes for my birthday, and I decided to show them off at the park. It felt warm in the sun as I walked toward the direction of the park, but whenever the breeze blew it felt a little cold. I was walking in the direction of an underpass that I spray-painted in regularly.

Unfortunately, to get to the park I had to go through the tunnel, which put me at risk of rival gang members driving by.

As I moved down the street, I noticed a car that had gone by me earlier was now stopped ahead, just before the overpass. I had a bad feeling about the situation and I was almost positive the car belonged to a rival gang member. Suddenly, both the passenger and driver's side doors opened up and two guys stepped outside of the car. I froze in place. I felt like I was in one of those western movies and we were both supposed to draw guns, except I did not have a gun and I assumed they did. Those few seconds seemed endless. I reached down and touched my jeans pocket, remembering I had my little screwdriver that I carried for protection when I spray-painted. I never really expected to have to use it to kill someone.

Finally, the driver yelled at me, "Where you from ese?"

I gave him my gang's name and he yelled back his. The only problem was that his gang was my gang's direct rival. I knew I only had one option, and that was to run.

I turned on my heels and ran like a track star back towards my brother's apartment. I could feel the weight of my new shirt, large over-sized jeans, and bulky sneakers. Not the best outfit for a life-saving run. I momentarily glanced behind me, only to see the two guys had abandoned their car and began chasing me on foot. No one would go through that much trouble just to beat someone up. These guys planned to kill me. I could feel it.

Over the last year, I had gained a lot of practice outrunning danger. I could feel the gap between my enemies and me growing smaller. I did not have time to be afraid or imagine what they might do once I got caught. I ran faster, back towards my brother's place. Finally reaching the building, I ran straight into the apartment and locked the door shut. Immediately, I yelled for Peter's girlfriend.

"Bianca! Bianca! I just got chased by some fools from the North Side!"

"What the hell are you talking about?" Bianca said, surprised.

"These fools hit me up and then started chasing me!"

When a gang member hits you up, it means they want to know what gang you are from. If the gangs are rivals, then one person is going to end up hurt or killed.

I peeked out the window and looked around, but did not see anyone. I began to relax. Bianca ignored me and walked back into the bedroom with my niece. I had the feeling she did not believe me, or else she was just so used to gang life that if someone was not bleeding, then who cared?

Not even ten minutes passed by before I heard keys in the door. I jumped up and Peter walked in the door.

"What's up?" Peter asked me.

"I was walking up to the park to go to the football game and these fools hit me up."

"Where at?"

"Right outside. I didn't even make it to the freeway underpass. I was walking and they slowed up, got out of the car, and hit me up."

"So what did you do?"

"I ran back over here and those fools were chasing me. But I made it in the house."

"Where were they from?"

"The North Side."

"Ahh, we'll bust those fools up. Don't worry about it. Let's go. I heard everybody is up at the park," Peter said nonchalantly.

Peter was not afraid of anything, and I felt better since he was home. Something about having an older brother around that makes you feel safer. Peter went in the room and asked my niece if she wanted to come to the park, but she decided to stay home with her mom. We rolled out of the apartment. The car was parked in the narrow driveway just in front of the place. Peter walked ahead of me as we drifted toward the car. I looked around and did not see anyone on the street. Peter walked around the car and got in on the driver side. I pulled open the heavy car door and flopped into the front seat. Just as I was shutting the car door, I heard POP! POP! POP! It took me a moment to recognize the sound of a gun. However, the sound of bullets hitting the car was undeniable.

"Shut the door! Let's go! Let's go!" Peter shouted.

Everything was happening so fast. I looked around and didn't see anyone, but I realized the shots were coming from over the wall. Just as I slammed the car door and Peter skirted out the driveway, I felt something prick my arm. My left arm involuntarily shot up in the air. I was confused by what was happening, but suddenly my arm started flailing around and burned like fire.

I shouted, "I'm hit! I'm hit!"

Peter quickly glanced over to check where I had been shot. Next, he focused his attention back to the street and wildly drove me to the county hospital. As I looked out at the people in the streets, I felt like I was in the *Matrix* movie.

I had never been so happy to see the big, bright red letters that spelled out "Emergency." Peter hopped out of the car and ran in to get a nurse. I thought they would come out with a gurney. Instead the nurse hurriedly had me walk directly to a bed in the back. She cut off my brand new jersey and immediately assessed my wound. The nurse was too good at this. I figured she had seen a lot of gunshot victims at this hospital.

"You're so young! You're so young!" she kept saying, shaking her head from side to side.

I had no control over my arm and I could not feel anything. However, I was more worried about what my mom was going to say, rather than the fate of my arm.

It was not long before I heard my mom's voice in the hallway. I felt a pit hollowed out deep in my stomach. I swallowed hard, preparing for the worst. I quickly shut my eyes and put my head down, hoping my mom would think I was asleep. She rushed into the room, crying, relieved that she found me still alive. Immediately, I felt bad that she had to relive this moment as she had with my oldest brother, David. David died in this exact same hospital, probably the same room. I had no idea how she managed to arrive at the hospital so quickly, but I was not complaining.

Later, I found out that my god-sister, Tammy, was one of the first persons to find out I was shot. Tammy did not have many details to relay to my mom. Therefore, my mom had to drive to the hospital, thinking she might have lost a second son to gang violence. Fortunately, I was alive for my mom to tell me she would not allow anything like this to happen again. I was not sure what she meant, but I could tell she was very serious. I spent a little over a week in the hospital. The bullet pierced through my left upper arm and broke it, leaving it paralyzed. The doctor said I was lucky to be alive, and had the bullet hit me half an inch to the left or right, I would have been shot in the heart. He said I would recover after a while, with only a small scar.

I was in pain for the next several weeks. I would stay up late, enduring the discomfort, stewing in anger over someone trying to kill me. I became increasingly paranoid and refused to walk anywhere. But, I still had not learned my lesson. Before long, one of the homies would come by and pick me up. I still had my arm in a sling, and I was already hitting up the party circuit. The shooting had not slowed me down. Having a bullet wound made me a celebrity in my barrio. Getting shot was the worst thing that could have happened to me, because it only increased my rebellious attitude.

I got shot in October, and by December of 1989 I was back on the streets, with my arm in the sling. Everybody wanted to know what happened and what it felt like to get shot. I had earned a badge of honor and a level of respect that few had.

I had kept in touch with Laura, the girl I met a few months back when I was driving around with my homeboys. We talked on the phone every now and then. She had heard about me getting shot from other people in the barrio, but I could tell that unlike other girls, the violence did not impress her. One night, I was tired of being in the house and one of my homeboys stopped by and picked me up to go to a party. I had a feeling that Laura would be there and I kind of wanted to see her. We pulled up to the kickback in the homie's burgundy Monte Carlo. I wore a black jersey, black jacket, corduroys, and my black and white Converse. I felt good going back to hang out in the barrio.

I stepped into the party and my vibe was upbeat. Before the shooting, I was always a bit quiet and very laid back. However, the shooting had catapulted my notoriety. I felt like I needed to play up my new celebrity status. I was saying "what's up?" to everyone and answering all the questions when I saw Laura out of the corner of my eye. I pulled Laura off to the side and we sat down on a bench to talk. She asked me about my arm, but not in the kind of way that sounded like she was excited and caught up in the hype. Laura sounded more worried about my health. She asked me questions like how I planned to keep myself out of trouble. I wanted to avoid that conversation, and she could tell. That's when we kissed. In December of 1989, I kissed my future wife for the first time.

# CHAPTER 4

# TEXAS HOLD 'EM

M y partying and rebellious attitude was at an all-time high by early 1990. I was drinking and ditching school regularly. My mom had grown extremely tired of my behavior and all of the violent influences in our neighborhood. In the hospital, my mom had threatened that things were going to change, and those changes came quickly. When the opportunity came for my mom to move to Texas with her long-time boyfriend, she jumped at it right away, dragging me with her.

Part of me was excited to get out of the barrio. I lived in paranoia, thinking that the shooters might come back to finish me off. I thought my dad would be opposed to me moving, but for once he and my mom agreed that maybe getting me out of town and a change of scenery would do me good. My mom could not live with losing another son. Staying in the area was not an option for her.

Texas was flat and dry compared to California. I was used to seeing hills and mountains in the distance. Here in Texas, there were no hills and no mountains. Everything about Texas was different from the barrio. People dressed, spoke, and acted differently. Everything was spread out and far away from each other. There were not any buses in the neighborhoods. I guess they did not need them, since I never saw anyone walking anyway. The roads were long and the sun would drift high in the sky over the horizon until sunset. In my new neighborhood, instead of hearing cars bumping N.W.A., I heard country music. I was not even in town for a full week before I knew I would not like it here. I missed the barrio.

My mom was hoping I would adjust to my new life and make friends. I think she was hoping for a happy ending. She took me down to the local high school and got me signed up. I made sure to wear an outfit that oozed my barrio and proved I was from Los Angeles. I wore baggy khaki pants, an oversized jersey, and Nike Cortez shoes. My mom mentioned maybe dressing less like a cholo might help me in this new city. She reminded me that this was a new opportunity for change, but I ignored her.

Seeing the kids at my new school was a shock for me. Everyone had on tight fitted clothes and looked like something out of a Western movie. I could not figure out why everyone was so happy. I saw students walking around at lunch with cowboy hats on. I wondered if those kids were being punished and that was why they had on these dumb outfits. At my old school back in California, I was used to hanging out with Mexicans or only kids from my barrio. Schools in the barrio had lots of different races, even though each race mostly hung out with their own ethnicity. I naturally began looking for Mexicans to hang out with. Not only could I not find any Mexicans, but also I noticed that the school was filled with almost all white people.

Between my clothes and my ethnicity, I stuck out like a sore thumb. I was no longer cool in Texas. I spent so much time in the barrio earning my place with my homeboys to become cool. I never thought what it would be like in other places where no one knew about my gang. Needless to say, I was having a difficult time adjusting to my new surroundings. My mom suggested I take the school bus, thinking that it would help me meet other kids.

My first few weeks on the school bus, no one really talked to me. Aside from "excuse me" as someone was trying to get by, I never had anyone to talk to like the other kids did. Instead of trying to fit in with the crowd, my attitude just grew worse. The plan my parents had for me was backfiring. The last thing I wanted to do was fit in with these kids who were judging me.

One afternoon on the bus I caught a couple of kids staring at me and laughing. I tried to keep my cool, but I was done being nice. These kids had no idea who I was and where I had been. Finally, one of the kids pointed at me.

"You better put your finger down before I bust you in your snot-box," I yelled.

Back in the neighborhood, "snot-box" was a term we used all of the time, a term that referred to someone's nose. Unfortunately, instead of sounding intimidating, the kids got a kick out of my terminology. I heard a girl shout from the middle of the bus, "Snot-box? What's a snot-box? Who says snot-box?" The whole bus was laughing. I went to class vowing I would not be in Texas much longer. I planned to do whatever it would take to get back to Los Angeles.

The kids made fun of me for a few days about the "snot-box" incident. But soon they moved on to laughing at some other kid's poor misfortune. Eventually, I made a friend with the one Mexican kid in the school named Carlos. I was happy to have someone to hang out with on occasion. Carlos was really nice and he was nothing like my friends back home. One day after school he invited me to an event at his church. I was surprised he wanted to go to church and no one was forcing him. I believed in God and definitely feared Him, but I was not at a place in my life where I prioritized church. My dad was into church.

I remember as a kid he would make me pray over my meals and before I went to sleep at night. But my mom wasn't a church person.

I decided to take Carlos up on his offer to go to church with him. I figured at worst I would be bored, but at least I would have some company. However, it turned out that I really liked the service. I felt like everything the pastor was saying was specifically meant for me to hear. I was so excited that I thanked Carlos for taking me when he dropped me back off at home. I walked in the house and no one was there. I wanted to tell my mom about some of the things I learned in church, but she was not around.

Next, I decided to call Laura. We were still keeping in touch even though I had moved away. I grabbed the phone off of my nightstand and called her up.

"Hey, girl! It's me," I said.

"Hi, Brian. What's up? You sound really excited."

"I am! Remember I told you that dude, Carlos invited me to church? "

"Yeah, I remember."

"Well, I went and it was really good!"

"That's great, Brian! I'm happy for you. You've sounded kind of down lately. I'm glad you had a good time!"

"Laura, do you have a Bible? I want to read you something. Find First Corinthians chapter 13 verses 4 through 7," I concluded.

Eventually, Laura found her Bible and I read the scripture to her. She sounded like she really liked it. Something happened to me that night at church. I had heard this Bible verse before, but somehow right then the words on the page seemed to touch me. I felt like I could really understand for the first time what God was saying to me personally. It was ironic that the first verse to impact me talked about love. "Love is patient, love is kind. It does not envy, it does not boast, it is not proud." This statement was everything that my gang was not. Although, the teaching did not grow inside of me immediately, a seed was definitely planted.

I hung out with Carlos and talked to Laura on the phone for the rest of the school year. As summer approached, I was looking forward to visiting home. My dad agreed that I could come out for the summer. However, I never planned on going back to Texas.

As soon as school was out for summer, I boarded a plane for Los Angeles. I had never loved the sound of wheels hitting the pavement more than the wheels of my airplane as it landed at LAX. I hit the ground running. My dad could not keep track of me. Within days, I was connected back with all of my homeboys from the barrio. Every time I walked into a party, I received so much love. All I would hear was, "What's up, homeboy?" followed by heavy handshakes and pats on the back. Now I had even more clout than before I left. People saw me as the guy who survived the bullet wound and now I had traveled beyond what we knew there in the barrio. I felt tougher than ever. I started dressing in as much gang-affiliated clothes as I could possibly put on. I was hanging out all of the time and never listened to my dad. My father literally tried to restrain me from leaving the house once, but his strong-arming me did not work. I always managed to get out of the house, and I even started running away.

I was a master at running away from home. Every time I didn't get my way at home, I would leave to go to the streets. In fact, I had a crew of homeboys who were runaways too and lived on the streets with me. We would sleep in the park, abandoned homes and even abandoned diesel trucks.

Living on the streets eventually became tiring. I would be walking late at night in the cold, dreaming about my warm bed at home, but too prideful to go back. Then a lot of my homeboys started to get tired of seeing me around all the time. They knew once I connected with them,

I would be with them all night because I had nowhere else to go. On top of that, I always had to watch my back, because there was a full-scale gang war going on. The early '90s were crazy times, drive-by shootings all the time.

One night as I was spray-painting my barrio's name on the side of the wall, the police busted me. They handcuffed me and started to ask me questions about a gang-related shooting that took place that night. I knew enough about the street life not to say anything.

"Where's your other homeboy?" the police officer yelled at me.

"I don't know who you're talking about," I answered.

He immediately smacked me in the face with his huge flashlight. I was stunned, but kept quiet. The officer took me to the station and booked me for attempted murder in connection with that shooting that took place in a rival gang's barrio.

I didn't realize the seriousness of my situation until I woke up the next morning in Los Padrinos Juvenile Hall. Wow. I was facing attempted murder charges. But almost everyone I was surrounded by was too. I remember being in my cell late at night, trying to strike a deal with God.

"God, if You let me out, I promise I will go back to church."

Several days later, I learned the District Attorney was releasing me because there was not enough evidence to prove I was involved in the shooting. My arrest for attempted murder and release fueled my pride, rebelliousness, and ego even more. I didn't fulfill my promise to God. Instead, I lied to Him and went back to the streets.

My parents could not handle me anymore. I bounced between Texas and California several times over two years. By 1992, I had enough and ran away from Texas back to California for the last time. I had masterminded a plan to get from Texas to Los Angeles in my new used card, a white 1980 Chevy Monte Carlo. When the day came for me to leave, I bought a spare tire for my car with money I had saved up and headed for the highway. I never said goodbye to my mom or the few friends I had made. I drove and drove through the night. After hours of driving, I realized I forgot to bring food and it was way too late to turn back. What a genius I was. I had spent the last of my money on gas and the spare tire. I decided to keep driving.

When I became tired, I pulled over to the side of the road to sleep in my car. I drove through rain and a hailstorm passing through Texas, New Mexico, Arizona, and finally California. It took me two-and-a-half days to reach Los Angeles. I was starving. I had scrounged up enough change in my car to eat a hot dog during the trip. I was without any energy left. My car and I were both without fuel by the time we reached the barrio.

I entered the barrio full of excitement, though. I had my own car now and I would be able to hang out with my homeboys whenever I wanted. As luck would have it, as soon as I drove into the barrio, my brother Peter was driving out. I was astounded, wondering what were the odds of this happening? I hoped that Peter had not seen me, so I hurriedly turned the corner and parked my car at my homeboy Midget's house. The moment I got out of my car, I could sense someone walking quickly towards me. I turned to face Peter.

"Why did you leave Mom?" he shouted angrily.

Peter swung his fist at my face, but I was quick and missed the punch. Surprising myself, I swung back at Peter and hit him in the face. But I was too much of a lightweight to fade him. Next thing I knew, we were moving in circles, swinging at each other. Finally, Peter became frustrated and walked away, but not without kicking my car door first. I was indifferent to the whole situation.

"To hell with Peter!" I thought, annoyed.

I wiped my face, straightened my clothes, and walked into Midget's house, hoping for something to eat.

I did not go to my dad's house, fearing he would make me return to Texas. I began to live on the streets again. I drove around in my car all day and would either sleep in the car or at a homeboy's house. I roamed the streets night after night, envisioning a warm bed and cooked dinner. It was like when I was little all over again, just riding around aimlessly at night. Except now I had no home to go to.

One night I went to a house party where everyone was hanging out. I recognized one of Peter's friends, who we called Capone. I had not seen Capone in a while. I heard through rumors that Capone had become involved at church. Therefore, I was surprised to see him at the party. Capone came over and we reconnected, catching up and sharing stories. Finally, Capone asked me if I wanted to hit up a spot on Whittier Boulevard where other friends from our gang hung out. I had nowhere else to be and thought I lucked out with his invitation. We seemed to drive around in circles until finally I told him to forget about the plan to go to the Boulevard. Capone suggested we go back to his family's house and I could spend the night there.

The next morning, Capone revealed the real reason he invited me out. He asked if I wanted to go to church with him that morning. I did not hesitate in saying yes. Capone had already done more for me this day than most of my homeboys had done. Plus, I would have somewhere to be and maybe get lunch, too.

I walked into the church and noticed that everyone was singing really loud. I stood there, anxiously waiting for the singing to stop. I was overwhelmed by the people raising their hands to the sky and felt uncomfortable when they cried or shouted out. I did not know if I was supposed to sit, stand, or sing. I just stayed quiet, trying not to look around. After what seemed like an eternity, the pastor walked to the front of the church. I breathed a sigh of relief after he said we could be seated. I should have saved my sigh, because once the message was finished, Capone urged me to go forward when the pastor called people to come forward if they wanted to receive Jesus. I could feel people staring at me. They seemed to be rooting for me, yet I was not sure why. I went forward and the pastor prayed over me. I went back to my seat. I could feel Capone staring at me. I assumed he expected me to be crying, or something. However, I was void of emotion. I will admit, after that church service I got tired of living on the streets. Eventually, I moved back into my dad and grandmother's house.

Living with my dad was not a picnic. He was still conservative and strict. I was anything but agreeable when it came to rules. My father and I constantly lived in a state of tension. He wanted me to listen and I never did. One evening, the tension came to a boiling point. In my usual routine, I prepared to leave the house late one night. My father told me I was not allowed to leave. I looked at him and continued walking towards the door as if he had not said anything at all. Within seconds, before I could turn the knob, my father wrestled me to the grown. Panting and out of breath, he told me he did not want me in the streets. I could see the anguish in my father's face, but I ignored him. I lay there under the weight of his frustration and hurt, and I ignored him. I would not back down. My grandma rushed into the room, frown lines covering her face, full of worry and concern.

"If he wants to go that bad, let him go," she said.

Both my father and I ended our struggle on behalf of my grandmother. I walked out of the house, knowing that was a pivotal point in my relationship with my dad. I felt free. I knew he couldn't hold me down any longer.

It was not long before my behavior got me arrested again. One night, I was out with a few of my homeboys and I got bored. I grabbed a can of spray-paint and decided to wander around by myself. I found an untouched wall on the side of a Kentucky Fried Chicken. I started spraying as usual, but suddenly a cop car drove past, and when I looked up we made eye contact. I took off running, but the cop car caught up to me quickly. I was arrested and taken back to the Los Padrinos Juvenile Hall. The police called my father and I was afraid to see him, especially after the big fight we had just gone through.

My dad showed up and had me released. The ride home in the car was very quiet, highly uncomfortable for me. He did not seem mad, more so worried. In that moment, I only cared about myself. My dad's grief was the last thing on my mind. I am sure my father thought that an evening in juvenile hall would make me rethink my actions. Instead, I felt more entitled to behave badly. I was racking up a gangster's resume: shot, jailed, violence, defacing of property, and runaway.

"Why stop now?" I asked myself.

Being a part of a gang is a way of life in the barrio. Once I decided to become a gang member, I ultimately signed over my life in exchange for this call of death, even though that wasn't my initial intention. At first I just wanted to party and have fun, but I soon learned I couldn't pick and choose what aspects of gang life I preferred. Gang life was all about loyalty and it was for life, so I thought. My biggest act of loyalty to my barrio would soon come–at a great price.

## CHAPTER 5

# TAKE A LOOK AT THESE STREETS, BOY!

In the spring of 1992, I was still living at my dad's house and partying elsewhere all the time. I met a new kid in the barrio named Andrew. He was a year younger than me and wanted to join our gang. We started hanging out. He was cool and I liked having someone I could show the ropes to. By the time summer rolled around, I still had a car and we would ride around most of the day. I rarely went to school, or would ditch just before lunch. Therefore, I had to make up some class in summer school. Most of the time, Andrew and I never did much of anything. We would ride around, go to kickbacks, drink, or spray-paint on walls on occasion. We never did anything out of the ordinary for us, but that would soon change.

One day, I went to pick up Andrew, and he told me one of his friends had brought a gun to his summer school class. Andrew thought he could probably get his friend to let him borrow the gun. I was excited to see it and urged him to get it. I thought it would be cool to show off the gun to my girlfriend.

Eventually after retrieving it, Andrew stopped by and let me borrow the gun. The gun was archaic. It reminded me of something out of an old western movie. The barrel was sawed off and only allowed one shot. Having a sawed off shotgun made it compact and easy to hide in my car. I would still get paranoid on occasion since I had been shot. Having the gun with me made me feel secure.

Excitedly, I called Laura and told her I had a surprise for her. I thought she might be impressed. Fact of the matter was that she was not only unimpressed, but she was angry with me. After I called her, I immediately drove over to her house. I pulled up in the driveway and she came outside and walked up to the car. I got out to hug her.

"Hey, girl! What's up?" I said.

"Um, nothing, was just doing some homework," she said. "So where's my big surprise? You got me excited on the phone. I figured you were making up for the fact that I haven't seen you in a few days."

I turned back to the car and slowly pulled the gun out from the car panel.

"Check this out!" I said as I showed her the gun.

"Brian! Oh my God! What were you thinking?!" she said. She was angrier than I had ever seen her before. "Get rid of that gun! Why do you have that?!"

"Relax! Why are you tripping?"

"How could you bring something like that to my house?"

"I don't know. I thought you would want to see it," I said as my shoulders began to slump.

"Are you out of your mind? I don't know what you are doing with that gun, but you need to get rid of it. I don't know what you're getting into, Brian, but this is not cool. This is not you and it's definitely not me," my girlfriend said with confident disgust.

I started to put the gun away. I was afraid to make her any angrier.

"Look, I thought you were coming over here to bring me a gift or just see me. Not to show me a gun! Brian, that gun could get you or someone else killed. I don't know where you got it from, but promise me you're going to get rid of it."

"I planned on giving it back later today."

"Promise me!"

"I promise. Don't worry. I'm not going to keep it."

"Okay." She looked away sadly.

I kissed my girlfriend on the forehead as she looked up at me. I could see worry in her eyes. We were only sixteen, but plenty of girls in Los Angeles attended funerals for their boyfriends.

"I love you. I'll take care of the gun. I will get rid of it," I said.

"Okay, well I have to go back inside and finish my homework. I love you, Brian."

"I love you, too," I said.

Stunned by my girlfriend's reaction, I drove home with plans to meet up with Andrew to give him back the gun. However, having the gun secretly stashed in my car made me feel very proud. I felt a sense of honor that I had matured within my gang. I was my own man, not just David and Peter's little brother. Most importantly, I felt safe. There had been an increase of shootings and violence in our barrio. The gun gave me security and power.

I still held on to the gun for a few more days. Soon, more and more people from my barrio knew I had it hidden in my car. I was gaining more respect. The newly found confidence was feeding my ego, and my ego was starved for attention. As the days passed, I felt less obligated to return the gun to Andrew. No one had been hurt. I kept it in my car and never planned to use it. If anything, the gun was keeping me safe just because people knew I had it. I started to relax to the idea that I would keep the gun in my car.

Just as quickly as I was resigned to keeping the gun, I was pulled over by the police while driving. I looked like a gang member, so the cops always pulled me over. A couple of my friends from the barrio drove by and stared at me, knowing I had the gun in the car. We all assumed I was going to jail for possession of a concealed weapon. My heart started to beat fast. My first thought was "Why didn't I give the gun back?" However, suddenly the cops came back and told me that I could go. I could not believe my luck! They did not find the gun, although they were looking for something. I stood up from the sidewalk and hopped back in the car and headed to a homeboy's house. I began rationalizing keeping the gun, especially now that the police had not found it in my car. I put my music up loud and decided to cruise through the barrio as a sort of victory parade.

Two weeks had passed by since showing the gun to my girl-friend. I felt like all the drama had died down. I still had the gun in my car, but did not think much about it. On a hot day in July, I should have been headed to summer school, but instead I decided to ditch with Andrew. We headed over to a high school near a rival gang's barrio. It was pretty typical for kids to cruise around with loud music blaring from their cars, especially during the summer. On our way to the high school, we cut through the rival gang's barrio because I needed to turn around.

As I was driving out of the street, I noticed that someone spray-painted our rival gang's name on one of the walls. I asked Andrew if he wanted to go with me to grab some spray paint so we could come back and cross it out. Crossing out another gang's spray paint in their own barrio is the ultimate sign of disrespect. Andrew agreed with me, so we headed out to pick up the paint and returned to the same barrio just a few minutes later.

Ice Cube's "Death Certificate" album was playing on the tape deck. As we drove back into the neighborhood, to our surprise, there were a group of gang members outside, hanging out in front of a house. They were our rivals. This gang and ours had a long history of violence toward one another. Recently, they shot up one of our houses, where my little niece lived. It was crazy, because way back in the days, we used to be the same gang. But not in my generation and not today. It was all out war. The plans to spray-paint on the wall changed fast.

"Hey, you see them?" I said as we passed them by and arrived at the corner. "It's too dangerous to get out to spray-paint on the wall now," I thought out loud.

"Should we shoot at them?" Andrew responded.

What seemed as a long moment passed.

"Yeah, let's blast at them," I said.

I slowly drove around the block, headed back to our rivals. My hands were sweating and my breathing became slightly shallow. At the same time, I reached for the gun in the side panel. I handed it to Andrew and turned up the radio. I knew this was wrong. But my loyalty for my barrio overrode any type of morals left inside of me. We only expected to create chaos. I do not think either of us expected someone to die. I remember the song had a tribal beat and the base was pumping, causing my heart to beat faster. I had said yes to this, but I did not want to see what happened next. That was the fear raging in me.

"BAM!"

That was it. One loud shot and Andrew, who had been leaning out of the car as I was pulling up, sat back down and faced forward. I looked in my rearview mirror, and the further we drove the harder it was to make out any faces. People were scurrying like ants. Within moments, guys in a car from the scene were chasing us. I was afraid. My adrenaline was pumping. I drove hard and turned corner after corner. I could not out-run them because my car was old and too big to drive at high speeds. I drove and turned left, drove and turned right, and then again. This went on until I looked in the mirror and saw no one was following us anymore. I pulled over to look at Andrew.

"Did you hit someone?"

"Yes."

"Are you sure?"

"Yes."

"Damn!"

Shaking, I drove Andrew home and told him to stay there and not to talk to anyone. Eventually, I made it back to my dad's house. Every car, every turn, every man, woman, or child who looked at me, I thought, "They know." Paranoia was consuming me. Every noise was someone coming after me.

I walked into the house. My grandma looked at me with her eyebrows furrowed and lines of worry hugging her eyes. I walked past her and straight into my room to lie down.

I could not deal with the panic. I tried to desperately rationalize what we did in my mind. "Those are our enemies. They would have shot at me first if they could." I figured sleep would make me feel differently in the morning. Man, was I wrong.

## CHAPTER 6

# SLIPPING INTO DARKNESS

<hr>

There is a story told of a man climbing up the side of a mountain. Halfway up, he came across a rattlesnake.

"Can you give me a lift to the top?" asked the rattlesnake.

"I can't do that," the man answered, "you'll bite me."

The rattlesnake continued to ask him. Finally, the man gave in.

"You promise not to bite me?" he asked.

"Yes, I promise," the rattlesnake answered.

So the man put the rattlesnake on his shoulders and carried it to the top. But when they got to the top, the rattlesnake turned around and bit him. The man was shocked.

"You promised that you wouldn't bite me!" he said as he died.

"You knew I was a rattlesnake before you picked me up," the rattlesnake hissed as it slithered away.

*****

I woke up abruptly, frightened. It felt like I was underwater, drowning without air. I could still feel the rattlesnake from my dream slithering. It took me a few seconds to realize it was my bedroom door that woke me up. I thought it was my grandma telling me it was time to get up for school. I quickly looked around and felt out of sorts. The morning had not made anything better. We used that stupid gun. I had no idea if the person who was hit was dead or alive. I wondered how long it would take the cops to find me, if they ever did.

It wasn't within a few seconds before "BOOM!" my bedroom door was knocked in, off of its hinges. Suddenly, two policemen ran through the door with their guns raised and pointed. Now I was the hunted.

"Get down! Get down!" they yelled as I was forced to the ground. As they cuffed me, I swiveled my head around, catching one last glimpse of my room. As I was being escorted out of the bedroom, my family was crying in the living room on the couch.

"What did you do?" my grandma cried aloud.

I lowered my head in shame as I was escorted to the police car that was in front of the house.

The handcuffs were tight. I did not like the feeling of being snatched out of my home and my body being forced into this shameful posture of surrender. The entire neighborhood was outside of my grandmother's house. It was not even 7:00am and the entire block seemed to be buzzing and watching me. I did not make eye contact with anyone specific. The street was lined with cop cars. Officers with their hands near their guns. I could not believe this entire setup was for me. This was something I would see on television on those old cop shows I watched when I was little. Watching everything happening around me, I quickly realized that my life was the nightmare.

As the policeman pushed his hand on my head to force me in ducking down into the car, I took one last glance down the street.

In the distance, I saw my father. He was being kept away from the house. My dad worked the graveyard shift. I assumed they intercepted him before he arrived at home. I wondered, when he turned the corner and saw all of that police presence, if he automatically knew it was for me. I had become the son he had been warning me about. I was still dressed in my shorts and t-shirt that I had slept in overnight. I did not have shoes on. I no longer had rights. The plastic seats of the cop car felt cold on my skin. The seats were firm and stiff. The officer slammed the car door with a heavy thud. I sat back in the seat, staring through the holes in the screen separating me from the officers. I gritted my teeth and shut my eyes tightly.

There was a roar in me rising. I had an anger that could not be quieted. Everything in my life so far had led up to this caged existence. I felt my shoulders tighten. I wanted to pound my fists or punch a wall, but I could not because my hands no longer belonged to me. I was property of the State of the California: wanted, hunted, caught, and caged. My anger and aggression did not allow me to focus on the crime. I found it hard to focus on anything past my anger. My attitude was a distraction from the true hurts and real pain that surrounded my crime.

I took a deep breath, opened my eyes, and sat back firmly against the back seat. Slowly, the black and white police car began to pull away from my grandmother's house. It felt like being in a funeral procession. I was the dead man and this cop car my coffin. I was alive to watch my own death. People were staring into the car as if staring at a hearse. The looks of disgust, disappointment, disapproval governed the faces of my neighbors. Unfortunately, no one had the look of surprise. As we began to turn out of the neighborhood, I saw my uncle's car turning onto the street. His face looked perplexed and full of curiosity. Just as we were making the turn to exit, my uncle and I made eye contact. Finally, someone looked surprised to see me in the cop car! As we turned out of the barrio onto the main street, the detective in the passenger seat turned his face just enough so that I could see his profile.

"You better take a good look at those streets, boy," he said, "'cause you'll never see them again!"

I was only sixteen, and was unable to comprehend the concept of "never." I did not understand what that meant. How could I never see my grandmother again, or my family? I wondered if this officer was just trying to scare me. My only defense was my attitude. With my hands tied behind my back, I was helpless. I stared at the officer with indifference in my eyes and my eyebrows furrowed. Anger and hostility were my only refuge. I refused to cry.

I was taken to jail and placed in the juvenile section. I wore the orange jumpsuit, which indicated I was a high classification case for murder. The police questioned me for hours. They asked me the same questions over and over in every possible fashion. I offered no information. By now, I had been officially in the gang for three years. In gang life, three years was a long time. I also had witnessed enough of gang life, because my siblings were in gangs since I was very young. I knew from their stories and my own experiences that the police would question me, telling me things that Andrew supposedly did or did not say. I knew to keep quiet and wait for a lawyer. Andrew was new to our barrio. I wondered if he had been caught, and if so, how was he faring? After my first three days locked up in a room, I was moved to a regular building.

The judicial process is very long. It is not like you see on *Law and Order*. On those shows, a crime is committed and before the hour is up, a person has a trial and is sentenced. I would have months to spend in jail, with time to think about everything that had happened. My father visited me as much as possible. He would always remain upbeat, telling me that "God's will will be done," and we would pray for leniency. Like any child, I believed my dad. He was so positive during this time that I held on to every statement of hope. However, my attitude still remained the same. I definitely had a chip on my shoulder.

Following multiple court hearings, I found out that I would be tried as an adult for my crime. I was arrested for one murder, one attempted murder, and illegal possession of a firearm. The law stated that if you were sixteen years or older and involved in a violent crime, you could be tried as an adult. Had I been tried as a juvenile, by law, I would have been released at twenty-five years old. However, the words of my arresting cop tormented me. Being tried as an adult made me realize that the possibility of life in prison existed. It was very possible that I would not see the outside world ever again.

Months had gone by since the crime. I spent my seventeenth birthday in jail. My bunk was next to a big window, which had a clear view of the moon at night. Thoughts of regret over my life would terrorize my mind. I could not sleep. The days were long on this journey and I was just scratching the surface.

Following the decision to try me as an adult, my court hearings were transferred from the Long Beach courthouse to the Compton courthouse. My anger, frustration, and fears rattled me daily, especially when I learned my crime partner was tried as a juvenile and would be released mandatory in a few years. I couldn't understand how the driver in a crime would do less time than the actual shooter. I talked back to the guards and got myself in fights. My attitude had a profound consequence. Eventually, I was kicked out from Central Juvenile Hall and moved to the Los Angeles County Jail, Juvenile Hall section, one of the toughest and most barbaric jails in the USA.

According to the Los Angeles County Probation Department, "2,000 to 2,200 juvenile defendants are held in custody at one of the three juvenile halls (Central, Los Padrinos, and Nidor in the Valley) awaiting court action or transfer to another facility. The L.A. Sheriff's Department receives custody of minors who are determined to be 'unfit' for Juvenile court and ordered housed at County Jail by the court." The L.A. County Jail is mostly for adults, but they had a small section for juveniles who were too rebellious to be housed in juvenile hall. I was now living among the worst of the worst young criminals in Los Angeles.

A guard placed me alone in a dark cell, with other juveniles nearby in adjacent cells. All of those in there were facing murder charges with life or double life sentences. There was a dark, heavy cloud of depression. The stench of hopelessness filled the room from wall to wall. Any sign of a heart lay dead on the floor, stomped out by the degradation of heinous crimes and a lack of any love to keep the heart beating. The walls were so thick, not even a smidgen of joy could break through. At times, the only sounds were the muddled moans of anxious men sobbing, or grown men defecating in the cell nearby. This was hell on Earth.

The county jail does not have windows. Again, I recalled my arresting deputy's final words: "Take a good look at those streets boy, 'cause you'll never see them again!" I went months without seeing the sun. There was a time I was housed in a room with fifteen other violent juveniles. This was a dangerous place. Inmates were not safe or checked on by guards. We were fed like wild animals. A guard would bring food on a big silver platter and place it down. He would watch us as we would rush to fight over the food. I saw so many savage beatings among prisoners.

After a few months, we were moved to one-man cells. It was dark and cold in our new section. Everyone stood up all night, yelling to one another through the bars. This world was diabolical. All of the inmates in this section were under eighteen. Each week, someone would head out to court and always return with a life sentence. All too often, young men returned with double-life sentences. I looked forward to my court date if it meant getting out of the L.A. County Jail, but knowing my fate was sealed with life imprisonment made me want to wait things out a little longer.

Dreadfully, in September 1993, more than a year since my arrest, I had my day in court. The guards came and chained me up early in the morning. I was handcuffed, shackled at my ankles, and driven to the Compton courthouse for my sentencing. The courtroom was filled with people, including my family. My dad sat as close to the front as possible. As I entered the courtroom, my dad's eyes were filled with hope. He comforted me with his smile. My father had really become my champion after all. My mother was so distraught with all that had happened, she was a ball of emotions and nerves, which was to be expected. I wondered if the victim's family was also present. I was led to my seat. The benches were hard and cold. Everything in the courtroom looked old and weathered, as if it had seen many cases like mine over the years. We all rose to our feet when the judge entered the courtroom. I was numb to what was happening.

I was told that the District Attorney was fighting hard to get me the most severe punishment that the law would allow. My family's lawyer argued that I was only sixteen at the time of my crime and that the Youth Authority's psychologist and experts who evaluated me deemed I was a person who could still change for the better. Information about my life and that of the crime went back and forth between the two lawyers like a volleyball. Finally, the game point was left in the hands of the judge.

The judge sided with the District Attorney's reasoning that my crime fit an adult punishment. She felt that if I were to ever leave prison that I would have to earn my way back to civilization by showing change and proven rehabilitation. I sat there dazed, not realizing yet that every moment since joining a gang led up to this judgment. The consequences of my decisions and behavior had cost someone's life and now I would receive my punishment.

Suddenly, just like that, the judge's hand rose high off of the desk into the air as her black robe cascaded down. I heard the sound of the gavel slamming into her desk.

"Mr. Warth, you are sentenced to state prison for the term of life."

I was in a fog. I know there was noise happening behind me, but in my haze I could not determine if the noise was laughter, cheers, sighs, or crying. However, I know regardless of who rooted for what, the sentence was stunning. I was paralyzed inwardly, not knowing what to do or say. I had not yet comprehended the depth of my fate. I even missed the portion of the sentencing when the judge added a year for the use of a gun.

Before I could be removed from court, the judge had already moved on to the next case. An older man stepped forward and was sentenced to three years in prison. The convicted man burst into tears. I was shocked by his response. I wondered, had he not just witnessed my own sentencing? The man sobbed uncontrollably. In the moment I was confused by his response, but soon I would experience my own breakdown as prison loomed ahead.

I arrived back at the dreaded County Jail in downtown Los Angeles by dusk. I was escorted back into my dreary cell and my handcuffs were released. I sat on my bunk and rubbed my wrists as the officer slammed the cell door. It felt like a weight of despair was crushing me. My body bent over as my face pressed against my knees. For the first time, I really realized the depth, hurt, and pain my crime had caused.

I had helped to ruin three lives: the victim's, my friend's, and last of all my own. And I couldn't even imagine the painful impact on all our families. I was not the first juvenile to receive a life sentence. I knew going into court that almost everyone in my jail tier received a life sentence, but I had never felt anguish before this moment.

My conviction was based on second-degree murder charges, not the original first-degree. But nothing felt comforting. Not even my father's endless positive attitude and call for prayer.

"Clearly, prayer did not work!" I thought. I started to get angry with God.

Hearing a noise coming from the hallway, I stood up and put my face against the cold metal bars to see who was out there. An old man slowly hobbled down the cement hallway, passing out something. I stepped back away from the gate. I did not want to see anyone. Regardless of my defensiveness, the old man approached my cell with Christian literature in his hand. He tried speaking kind words of encouragement. Clearly, the man did not plan on walking away, so I dropped my hopeless story on him.

"Mister, I just got sentenced to life in prison," I said, trying to shock him. "What can you do for me?"

After what I said, I expected the man to sigh or maybe move on. However, the old man did not move an inch. Instead, he did something so simple, yet powerful. The old man reached through darkness of the bars and grabbed my hands and prayed over me in the "Name of Jesus Christ." For the first time, tears began to rain down my young face like a hurricane. In my darkest moment, this stranger penetrated my heart with the love of God. Finally, something other than hopelessness had seeped through the walls and cracks of this jail.

Several days later, I had this strong and clear realization that sooner or later, whether it took ten, twenty or thirty years, I would wake up one day in prison with the thought, "Man, I wish I would have changed when I was younger." In my heart, I knew I did not want to wait. Even if I remained in prison forever, I wanted to die a changed man.

This realization, coupled with the reality of my terrible condition, drove me to my knees. I cried out to God for help. It wasn't even a prayer. It was more of a sigh, a grunt from severe emotional pain.

I turned eighteen years old in that cell. No party, or friends to send well wishes. I lived days fueled by sorrow and loneliness. To celebrate my birthday before the day went completely unnoticed, I threw a Snickers bar onto the walkway and watched as the other inmates on the tier fished for the candy with lines made out of ripped sheets and slippers tied to the ends. I spent each day in darkness with not much to live for. Imagine a 6'3" super-skinny teenager, with a shaved head.

I was awaiting transfer to the California Youth Authority (CYA). According to the state's definition, the CYA was a compilation of youth prisons that "provided education and treatment to California's youthful offenders up to the age of 25 who have the most serious criminal backgrounds and most intense treatment needs." But to us, the CYA was Gladiator School, a place where all the worst young gang members were housed and daily fought.

The judge had ordered that I spend time at CYA before being moved to state prison. There were many prisons facilities under the umbrella name of CYA, but I was excited to leave the County Jail and hoped for the possibility to see one of my brothers, who was housed at a CYA prison. Soon, I was transferred to Heman G. Stark Youth Training School in Chino (YTS), California. One thing was for sure; I certainly would not miss the L.A. County Jail.

My father and my girlfriend, Laura, visited me almost weekly. Ever since I was a kid, my dad would constantly tell me about Jesus. Honestly, those conversations would go in one ear and come out the other. Nothing ever stuck in regard to conversations about God and faith. However, my dad's efforts were not completely in vain. The book of Proverbs says, "Train up a child in the way he should go, and when he is old, he will not depart from it" (22:6).

I believe the seeds of faith he planted were inside of me, waiting for my heart to have the right condition for them to grow. As I began my initial journey of growth, I had not completely surrendered my heart to believing in Christ, but I had started reading the Bible and then something really strange happened.

Brian's prison ID

Brian & Laura at visiting, CYA

Brian & his dad at visiting, CYA

Brian in cell, CYA

# CHAPTER 7

# GLADIATOR SCHOOL

W hen an inmate arrives at a new prison, he or she is sent to the reception center. The reception center is nothing like a party reception. This is a building where an inmate goes through the intake process. This is the place where you undergo physicals and mental screenings. Inmates are housed in this building, sometimes up to a few months, until officers figure out the best place to put them. Officers have the job to make sure to house inmates in building and room situations that avoid racial or rival gang situations, to decrease violence within the prison.

During my time in reception at the YTS, I had one of the strangest life experiences. I was reading the Bible and my heart started to beat really fast. I clutched my chest, forcing me to put the Bible down. I was not hurting, but I was overwhelmed by the rapid heartbeats. I waited a few minutes, and picked the Bible up again to read. My heart started beating fast again. I slammed the Bible shut and closed my eyes tightly, taking a few deep breaths.

I got on my knees to pray. "God, I need help. Please send someone to help me serve You in the midst of this darkness." I finished my prayer and went about the rest of my day, not thinking much more of the experience. Two days later, God would remind me of my prayer. I was transferred out of the reception building to a room with one of the most well-known Christian inmates at YTS. He was at court when I was first escorted into the room. When he returned, I was seated. I looked up and a young Hispanic man walked into the room and extended his hand toward me.

"Hi, my name is Jojo." He smiled.

"I'm Brian," I said.

Little did I know, God was up to something with my new connection with Jojo.

Leaving the county jail felt like a dream come true because living there was horrifying. I automatically assumed that anything would be better than that place. CYA was experiencing many of the same problems as the county jail. From what I could see, overcrowding at many of the prisons, especially among violent offenders, created an eerie environment. At any time, brutal fights would break out. They called the CYA Gladiator School because of all the violence. Having a friend like Jojo was definitely an answer to prayer.

Jojo was a former gang member from one of the biggest gangs in the San Gabriel Valley part of Los Angeles. He too was sentenced to life sentence in prison for gang violence. Long before me, Jojo had decided to serve God. I had not yet completely sold out to Christ. However, I was attending church and I would sit in the chapel, listening to the preachers. I started reading Christian books too. I could feel my spirit getting stronger. My soul had been in darkness for a long time. I felt overwhelmed by this new feeling of commitment to things that were good in nature.

One night at church, I was sitting near the front when I began to have that heart experience again. I felt an urgency to make an open commitment to the Lord. I tried to shake the feeling, but I could not.

Soon the portion of the service came when the pastor announced, "If there's someone here tonight who wants to give his life to the Lord, stand up now." I began to panic. Standing up in this room full of young gang members was the last thing that I wanted to be doing. But somehow that rapid beating in my heart and something inside revealed to me that standing up in this moment needed to be done. It was an outward symbol to God and others, reflecting my commitment to Jesus and a new way of life. My mind may have not wanted me to stand up, but my heart would not let me stay seated.

I stepped up and surrendered my life to Jesus Christ that night. I surrendered my old way of thinking in exchange for a new way of life. No matter how difficult this new journey might be, I was committed to using the Bible as my example. I publicly gave my life to Christ in 1994 at eighteen years old in front of many gang bangers, drug addicts and thieves in prison. For the first time that I could recall, I was doing something right. My journey's course had changed directions.

In the outside world, accepting Christ is probably highly praised and folks are commended. On the inside, here in prison, safety is in numbers and those numbers are provided by your gang affiliation. I knew when I stood up in that chapel that it would be an open rejection of my gang, and possibly make me a target by others.

The next afternoon during our exercise time, I saw a guy I knew named Rico. Rico was from Northeast Los Angeles and we had become familiar since my original arrest. Since 1992, Rico and I continued to bump into each other in different facilities. When I saw him, I thought Rico would be a good person to share my story with. Nervously, not knowing how he would receive the information, I approached Rico. He was happy to see me and I shook his hand.

"What's up, Rico, man?"

"What's up, loco?"

Loco, the Spanish word for crazy. Another euphemism we used to address folks on the streets.

"How've you been?"

"I been all right man. Glad to be out of the county. Although, it ain't like none of these places is any better. You see that fool's face from the fight yesterday?"

"Naw, but I heard about it."

"That fool's face was jacked up. When he looks in the mirror he's going to see the fool that did that to him forever. Ain't no fixin' that!" Rico said laughingly. "Wassup with you?"

"Man, I'm excited!"

"About what? I know you ain't gettin' out!" He chuckled.

"I wish! Naw, man I been going to church and stuff."

"Yeah, I kind of seen you with some of the Jesus dudes."

"Rico, I wanted to let you know that I gave my life to Jesus Christ and I don't bang anymore," I said straight out.

"I'm happy for you, man. I could tell that something was different about you since we first met up." Rico smiled.

To my surprise, Rico did not say anything negative. In fact, he respected my decision and we continued our conversation. This gave me a boost of confidence. Not all of my encounters were as positive as with Rico's. However, as I grew in my faith, I learned to better deal with uncomfortable situations.

My dad was still visiting often. Our relationship also started growing. For the first time, I was taking part in mending our relationship. I recognized the part I played in the breakdown of what happened between us as a father and son. Taking responsibility for my actions became a trend in many areas of my life. I could not change the past. I would if I could. Nonetheless, I could work on being a better person and mending bridges I had torn down.

My father became actively involved in my rehabilitation. My mom still lived in Texas, but she would do her best to fly all the way out to see me when she could. I know my mom dealt with blame. She blamed herself for my lifestyle. To the contrary, I could never blame my mom for my mistakes. I had to take full responsibility for everything that had happened. I did not deserve this much support, but God continued to bless me, to show me that His love is unfailing.

My girlfriend, Laura visited me just about every week. Many times she would be the first in line, with my favorite banana cream pie. Back then, you could bring in food at visiting. Her support for me fed me hope in my dark world. God was also dealing with her as He was me. Laura eventually gave her life to Christ too and made a commitment to support me all the way. This was a huge miracle in my life.

YTS had a regular chaplain who oversaw the faith ministries. A new chaplain named Reverend Leonard Wilson-Banks Jr. had come on board. Chaplain Banks was a tall and hefty man with a heart for the work of God. As a young man, he had completed hard time in the CYA system as well as prison. Having been an inmate himself, he connected with just about everyone around him. He gave us direction, challenged us to be inspired, and taught us about seeking God's purpose for our lives. When Chaplain Banks arrived, there was a good feeling in the air. All of the usual dreary days and angry faces seemed to be a little lighter. A revival was beginning. Young men were changing their lives and proclaiming a commitment to God. Chaplain Banks helped us navigate the transformation from gang member to Jesus follower.

My eagerness to be immersed in things of the Lord became evident to Chaplain Banks. After watching me for a few months, he started using me to assist with odds and ends during our chapel services. I was filled with an irreplaceable fire for Jesus. I could not spend enough time reading the Bible. I knew deep in my heart that God was preparing me for something big. I knew that eventually God planned to use my passion for Him on a larger level.

Before long, Chaplain Banks appointed me as an armor bearer for the service. This meant that I was responsible to serve all the volunteer pastors who came from outside of the prison. During services, I led pastors to a quiet area and remained there with them while each prepared and meditated before delivering the sermon. Soon, Chaplain Banks would have me sit up front with him during chapel services. This gesture of faith in me only increased my passion to grow more into a man of God.

I began talking about Jesus wherever I went. If guys were suspicious about my true conversion from gang culture to a man of faith, I believe passion over time won them over. In my trade class, I talked about Jesus with anyone who would listen. Soon, everyone knew I was no longer part of a gang. One of my most memorable days at YTS was the opportunity to lead a young man to surrender his life to Christ. For weeks I had been sharing the Bible with this guy named Weasel.

"Jesus is coming back any moment, and I will be caught up in the air with him!" I constantly told him. I would jump in the air to illustrate my point.

Finally, one day, Weasel and I were standing on the second floor of a house in our vocational trade class and he asked, "How can I go with Jesus too?"

Quickly, I opened my Bible, turning to the book of Romans and read, "That if you confess with your mouth the Lord Jesus and believe in your heart that God has raised Him from the dead, you will be saved. For with the heart one believes unto righteousness, and with the mouth confession is made unto salvation" (10:9-10). I was so excited that I could not wait to tell Jojo that Weasel had surrendered to God!

The revival that had begun with Chaplain Banks was spreading. As more young men joined the faith, our team grew stronger. Many young gang members started to flock to the church. The most unexpected hardcore gang members began to seek Jesus. Society often wonders what God sees in a young gang member. The Bible teaches that God looks at the hearts of people, not at the outer appearance (1 Sam. 16:7). Everyone has qualities that the Lord can use, even gang members too. In gang life, members learn about commitment, loyalty, courage, and boldness. I was hoping to share with gang members that these same lessons, if used for God, would be character builders. God began to touch the hearts of gang members. He gave us purpose and redirected our strength toward him. The Bible shares, "The glory of young men is their strength" (Prov. 20:29).

A good example of strength was my friend, Nacho. He was from one of the largest gangs in West Los Angeles. He gave his life to his gang and ended up in prison with a life sentence at seventeen. I first met Nacho in our carpentry class in YTS. He showed an extensive interest in the Bible. In his zeal, he would actually try to argue with me about the Bible, and he wasn't even a Christian.

One day, Nacho was sent to the hole for having a knife in his cell. When I found out what happened to him, I knew this was the right time to share with him about God's love. I asked a guard if he would give Nacho one of my pocket Bibles, knowing he would not have anything else to do but read while in the hole. Even though Nacho had a lot of homeboys at YTS, none of them sent him anything while he was in the hole.

When Nacho received the Bible, he later shared with me that he was touched by the gesture, but most importantly touched by God's words. Nacho started attending church with us after leaving the hole. One night, just like me, he stood up in front of everyone to surrender to Christ. The entire prison was shocked to find out that Nacho gave his heart to Jesus.

I wish every day could have been as exciting as the day of Nacho's conversion. I was now twenty years old, and hundreds of us were locked up amidst pure madness. For inmates at any CYA lock up, it is almost impossible to keep out of trouble. Young men fight over every little thing. I too had a couple of close encounters with violence.

One day, this guy named Boo Boo asked if he could borrow my shoes since he had someone coming to visit him. It was standard in prison to try to look your best when someone came to visit you. Immediately, I wanted to say no. This was prison, and I had a feeling he wanted to test me by keeping my shoes. However, trying to put my faith into practice, I let him borrow my shoes. After his visit, I waited for him to return my Nikes, but of course he did not. I became angry.

I knew I could not let Boo Boo take my shoes. Prison is like living on another planet. If I allowed people to disrespect me, I could be putting myself in danger with everyone. Plus, I was not that strong in the Bible yet. I did not act immediately. Instead, I thought for a while about how to handle this dreadful situation. Eventually, when I knew Boo Boo was outside of his room, I went into his room and took my shoes back. I wondered if this would turn into a fight and how I would handle it. But when he saw me later wearing the shoes, he just tried to play it off as if he had planned to return them all along. I just grinned and thought, "Yeah, right!"

I was proud of myself for not completely reverting back to my old ways. For all of the people who had tried for years to help change me, Jesus had been the only one who could.

Within a few months, I was bombarded with another hard situation. Two guards called me into a back room. I sat down, wondering what was happening.

"How have you been holding up in YTS?" one guard asked.

"Fine," I answered.

"I need you to be strong because I have some bad news to share with you."

"What is it?" I responded in curiosity.

"Your grandmother has passed away."

I slumped down in my seat, cried and was overwhelmed with sadness.

Back then, if one got special permission, one could actually attend the memorial of a loved one who passed away. I found out I was going to see my grandma for the last time, my dad's mom, the one who helped to raise me. The guards came early in the morning to shackle me down in chains. Then they gave me an armed escort to see my grandma in the funeral home. As I stood over her, all I could think about was the many times she warned me about the lifestyle I was getting into while on the streets. I pictured her sad face, the morning I was arrested. Tears of regret and sorrow began to flow down my face.

Back at YTS, our Sunday church services started to get filled with people. We did not have enough room in the chapel and had to start using the auditorium. Chaplain Banks promoted me to a deacon and I began hosting the services. I even began sharing the messages. I remember practicing the week before delivering my first sermon. I prepared by preaching to the pictures on the wall in my cell. I titled the sermon "Spiritual Growth," and was determined to preach the message with all my heart. My heart was beating fast. The place was filled with prisoners, and there were pastors visiting from the outside community. After being introduced, I took a deep breath and walked to the podium with my Bible gripped in my sweaty hand. As soon as I began to speak, the power of the Holy Spirit fell on me, and by the time I was finished everyone was standing, shouting, and praising God. The pastors were stunned to hear me preach with such power, conviction, and passion. However, no one could have been more shocked than me.

I returned to my room that night a different person. God's plan for my life had become so much clearer at this time. I continued to preach to myself in my room, as well as digging deeper into the Bible. Chaplain Banks recognized a gift in me and started to help me develop it. I opened up for many different ministers and spoke in front of hundreds of prisoners at a time. God was forming me into a leader.

A man named Pastor Willoughby, from Echoes of Faith Ministries in Ontario, CA. came to our chapel to hold a series of revival services. He was an elderly man filled with faith and had a powerful testimony. We enjoyed all of his messages. I was hosting one of his services when I called him up to deliver the sermon. As I walked back to my seat, he called me back up in front of the church.

"The Holy Spirit told me that you are going to be a powerful end-times preacher," he said.

I was stunned. I walked back to my seat in a daze. Later that night, I sat on my bed, thinking, "Can God really use me?"

During this season in my life, God began to impress upon my heart a new vision for my life. I got the sense that God was telling me, "Brian, if you continue to serve Me and don't give up, eventually I will set you free from prison to impact the world with the Gospel." I took this vision to heart and started to prepare for it.

I spent almost three years within the CYA system. I was maturing and growing in Christ at YTS. God was doing a wonderful work in my life. By now there were ten to twenty Christians in almost every building. We were everywhere! We were in the classrooms, the barbershop, and even working in the visiting area. Also, during this period of growth, Jojo and I began teaching our own Bible class. We designed the curriculum and appointed Nacho and Weasel as our assistants. For the first night of class we had planned tests, and would award prizes to the students at the end of the course. We were so caught up in the excitement of the church that we forgot nothing is permanent in prison other than one's sentence.

One morning, the guards unexpectedly ordered a lockdown of all inmates with life sentences. I thought it was because of a big riot that happened earlier. Instead, a violent murder had taken place in one of the buildings. An inmate had beaten, stabbed, and killed a female prison guard. He proceeded to place her body in a trashcan and sneak it past guards to place her in a dumpster. He wanted to steal her facility keys. The guard's body was found two days later in a near-by landfill. The killing rattled the entire CYA system, but even more specifically YTS. Things would never be the same. Prisoners would receive no more leniencies with security measures. Then-Governor Pete Wilson signed a new law that called for the "lifers" to be immediately transferred to state prison.

Jojo had already been moved to another building. Nacho had become my bunkie for an interim period. We waited in our rooms for the staff to process our paperwork that would transfer us to any one of several adult prisons in California. There were hundreds of inmates that needed to be moved. Among those moving were many Christian brothers. We prayed and agreed that God was sending us out on a Holy Ghost mission to continue and spread the revival of Christ in the prison system.

It was time for us to put into action all the things we had learned in our time together. Our spiritual boot camp had come to an end. I yelled out from my room for the other brothers to pray for their bunkies and anoint them with oil. Nacho and I were ready to put in some work for the Kingdom of God. We thought we were leaving together, but God had another plan.

Large gray county jail buses, we called them Grey Gooses, came and were loaded with prisoners. Guards came to our hallway and began to prepare everyone for the transfer. To my surprise, I was one of five people left behind. I sat alone in my cell, confused, wondering what was happening. Finally, night fell and I knew I definitely was not going anywhere that night. Suddenly, I heard keys at my door and aggressive footsteps.

"Face the back wall!" yelled the guard.

I became concerned, wondering what was happening. Once the guard left, I turned around to see Jojo.

"Wow! What's happening?" I said.

Jojo walked in with a big smile. We were happy to be bunkies again, even if it was only to be for a short time. We found out that all of the prisoners with life sentences had already been transferred to prison facilities. There were only six of us left, including Jojo and me. Therefore, they moved him back to our building and into my cell. Jojo was my first and last Christian bunkie in the Gladiator School.

Brian's baptism, CYA

Brian & Jojo, CYA

Brian preaching for one

of the first times, CYA

## CHAPTER 8

# BACK SIDE OF THE DESERT

<br>

T he next morning guards came and shackled my wrists with chains and placed a chain around my waist. The handcuffs on my wrist were connected to the chain on my waist. Next, tight cuffs were placed on my ankles. Being 6"3 and only 140 pounds, I was gangly in stature. Maneuvering was difficult for a man of my build. Although, I suppose, that was the point of this exercise. I had to take baby steps and be guided as if on a leash to the bus. This was not the first time that I had been shackled for a transfer, but being shackled was a vivid reminder that I was a prisoner and not in control of my own life. Because of the crime I committed and my involvement in gangs, I had sentenced myself to animalistic treatment. By the community's standards, I was no longer fit to be a part of civilization. Prison was anything but civilized.

Jojo and I were shipped out to Chino State Prison, one of the oldest and most dangerous prisons in California. This would be the reception center where we would be housed for possibly a few months until authorities decided what prison we would be sent to. Upon arrival, Jojo and I were shocked to be placed in a section called Palm Hall, which among inmates is referred to as The Hole. Palm Hall is full of isolated cells dedicated to prisoners who have caused a disruption and are forced into solitary confinement.

We learned that because the staff murder in YTS was in close proximity to our work station, they put us under investigation for it too. This was a routine investigation, but it still didn't settle well in our minds. I was already in jail for murder, and I sure didn't want to be investigated for another one. This stressed us out big time.

I was only twenty years old when we arrived at Palm Hall. This place was no joke. It looked just like the movies, filled with older prisoners who were mad at the world. The cell was hot and dark, with a metal screen welded to the bars to keep an inmate from being stabbed through the bars.

I sat down and told Jojo, "God has to have us on a special mission."

I had to believe this was our purpose. Focusing on God's purpose rather than our fate kept us encouraged. Everything about our situation was very damning. We sat with puzzled faces late into the night. I prayed that God would reveal His plan for us. As if on cue, late that night we received a message from God.

"Who shall separate us from the love of Christ? Shall trouble or hardship or persecution or famine or nakedness or danger or sword?.... No, in all these things we are more than conquerors through him who loved us" (Romans 8:35-37).

My heart began to race with excitement. A prisoner whose voice was coming from somewhere below us had just quoted a Bible verse from the book of Romans.

"That's God speaking to us!" I shouted to Jojo.

Those words gave us strength. We would need it.

The prisoners in Palm Hall went to a small outside yard for an hour once a week. The yard was divided into four fenced areas. A guard with an assault rifle stood in a tower looking down on us. One day, unexpectedly, I heard a shout from the guard, "Get down! Get down!" I turned and was surprised to see a prisoner jumping up the fence. POP! POP!

POP! The guard began to shoot at him. I fell, face to the ground in the hot desert sun, hoping a bullet didn't ricochet off the wall and hit me.

Jojo and I remained in Palm Hall together for a month. By the time the guards arrived to take us to the main line, we could not have been more excited to get out of the dark, dreary wall of The Hole. The guards transferred us to a building called Madrone. We were no longer cellmates. Jojo was placed on the third tier and I was on the first. We would yell out to each other on occasion through the tiny windows that faced the tiers.

When I first arrived in Madrone, there was no one else in my cell. I set my stuff down and began praying over the walls. A short time later, my new cellmate walked into the small cell. His name was Crazy. He was large in stature, both in width and height. He had deep-seated roots in gang life, which could be read on the tattoos that littered his body and face.

"Oh no. What am I into now?" I thought.

"Where you from?" he asked me.

"I'm a Christian," I responded.

He looked shocked at first, as if he were reluctant to accept my claim of faith. However, soon he became interested in what I had to say. I told him about Jesus and God's plan for his life. The next night, we stayed up really late. I shared the Bible, from the book of Genesis through Revelation. Toward the end of the night, my new cellmate broke down in tears as he expressed that he was tired of living a sinful life. He even flushed his lighter down the toilet. Inside, I was praising God for what I saw.

I was craving the fellowship of a church service. I had not been to church since I left the Youth Training School. I heard from a few inmates that there would be a service held in the kitchen. My cellmate and I signed up to go and we ended up meeting Jojo there too. I badly wanted to share my testimony and boldly stood up, asking the minister if I could share. To my surprise, he firmly declined. But I was not discouraged. I sat back down and told Jojo that I believed God would make a way for me to share my story. I did not have to wait long. While the minister stood up to sing and play his guitar, a string broke. I nudged Jojo in affirmation of God's work. The minister continued trying to sing, but then another string broke. Finally, he realized he could not sing without the aid of his guitar. He put the guitar down.

"There's a brother here who asked to give a testimony, but I told him no. I guess the Lord wants him to speak today," said the minister.

I boldly walked in front of everyone. For the first time, I was speaking to not just a crowd of youth like back at the Youth Training School. I was now speaking to diverse generations of men who varied in their levels of crime. I swallowed away any fear and began to speak confidently. I passionately spoke about the revival God was igniting in prisons to restore men's lives. Before closing out my time, I invited everyone to a Bible study I was going to host in the yard. Now all I needed to do was actually plan the study.

It was actually my twenty-first birthday on the day I planned to teach a Bible study in adult prison for the first time. I prayed to God, asking for inmates to feel compelled to join me as I taught about Christ. This was all I wanted for my birthday. I was not sure if anyone would show up. It was highly racial in Chino prison, with lots of tension in the yards. Once I got to the yard, I sat in the middle of the grass and waited. At first, I thought no one was coming, but soon a few guys came out and I started teaching about "Power in the Name of Jesus." By the end of the study, fifteen men had joined the circle and we were varied in age and race. God granted my birthday request.

Remaining motivated in prison could be tough. Many of the days seemed to run into one another. Sometimes I had to ask what day of the week it was. There was still the constant threat of violence, and oppressive feelings of depression and gloom floating through the hallways. Jojo and I would always encourage each other. However, we eventually parted ways. He was sent to prison in northern California and I was transferred to Ironwood State Prison in the California desert, twenty miles outside of Blythe before the Arizona border.

For some reason, God loves to use the desert to prepare His people for their purpose in life. Moses was found in the desert. The Children of Israel spent forty years in the desert. Even Jesus Christ had His own desert experience. I was no exception.

The inmates and environment at Ironwood lived up to the prison's name. There were inmates there who had been in prison for over twenty years and might never be released. Ironwood has been featured in many documentaries for its progressive violence and deadly riots. There were many rumors that prisoners had been shot by guards. Ironwood was a whole different arena and I received severe pressure from other inmates to stop serving God.

I longed to attend church to receive the word and meet other Christians for fellowship. But the chapel at Ironwood was closed almost every day. Here, the Christians in the yard were segregated by race. My heart longed for brothers to come together. I tried the path that had worked at the Youth Training School and at Chino. I called a couple of meetings with brothers who I knew were Christian. I shared with them what the Lord was doing. I hoped this would bring them together. On the contrary, I was not well received. The inmates looked at me like a young Christian trying to do too much. My youthful passion caused several of the Christian brothers to swell up with envy.

Fortunately, not everyone resisted the ministry I was trying to apply. Several men encouraged me to keep trying, and said seeing me in the yard talking about Jesus inspired them. The young Christian inmates gave me the most support. At times, a few of us younger Christians would meet in the chapel and just praise and worship God. On different days, we would walk around the track in the yard and look for people we could share the Gospel with. Sometimes we would bring someone back to the chapel and pray over him. We counted on the power of God to deliver the people. It would always humble me to see hardened criminals crying like a baby because the Spirit of God was cleansing them and lifting their burdens away.

As I remained faithful to God, my life began to be restored. God strengthened me by giving me a beautiful wife. At this point, I had already been incarcerated for six years. My father still made his regular visits, as well as my mom when she could fly out from Texas. The one person who did not have to come, but always did was my girlfriend, Laura. She was so faithful visiting me every week, no matter what facility where I was housed. Laura was my anchor. I could share my heart with her in person or through our letters. Her smile always gave me hope. Laura had become a Christian in the time I was in prison. Her faith had developed equally to mine, if not, her passion might have out matched mine! Laura was faith-filled and constantly reminding me of God's word. While I worked to encourage brothers on the inside, Laura worked from the outside to encourage me that one day we would be together again.

We were in love and had known each other since we were thirteen. Over the years, we had approached the subject of marriage, but Laura wanted to make sure that I had completely surrendered my gang habits to God before she would be willing to make that kind of commitment. Now that the years had passed and we were both grounded in our faith, we were ready to take the next step in our life's path. Although marrying a lifer inmate is extremely unconventional, Laura had faith that I would be released one day to have a family together.

Laura and I married in 1997. A prison wedding is very different than what I assume people experience on the outside. I had to have the necessary paperwork filled out. Laura, along with my dad, came out to the prison. That morning I woke up excited. I put on my best prison clothes, and had them ironed and prepared. I waited nervously in my cell for my name to be called. Finally, my name was called and the guards opened my cell and handed me a pass. I had to exit the building to get to the yard. I headed over to the visiting hall where I saw Laura dressed up so pretty. A minister authorized to marry us began a quick non-denominational service. At the end of the ceremony, we were allowed one short kiss.

When I arrived back at my cell, my Christian brothers surprised me with a reception. We shared Top Ramen noodles and one of the brothers gifted me with a Strong's Concordance Bible. There were no frills, but this was the best day of my life.

Laura later sent me a letter that read, "To the man of my dreams, this was the day we united as man and wife. I was blessed to be given the most wonderful man a woman could ever hope for. I will always love you with more than all my heart! Love, your wife, Laura Warth."

I was an inmate at Ironwood for one year. I was able to break through the iron cloud and minister to many inmates. Prison is full of hurting people who need someone to reach out to them with the comfort of the Holy Spirit. Many inmates just need a caring person to help them get back on the right track.

Shortly after my twenty-second birthday, in 1998, I was transferred to Chuckwalla Valley State Prison. Chuckawalla is just adjacent to Ironwood Prison. Both prisons are a little over 200 miles from Los Angeles. Chuckawalla is a lower-security prison and holds thousands of inmates with shorter termed prison sentences. Instead of cells, we were housed in open cubicles with ten to sixteen people in each cube.

Arriving at Chuckwalla was a traumatic change for me. I had been in a cell for so long that I was overwhelmed to be placed in a dorm setting. There was no privacy there at all.

I walked into the dorm and put my clothes on my bunk and lay on the mattress. I was trying to calm myself and adjust to all of the noise and movement. I quietly watched how things were run, studying the environment. A few inmates asked me what I was there for and were shocked to find out that I was the youngest inmate there with a life sentence. I stayed close to my bunk out of fear and figured I would begin my adventure the next day.

The next morning, I immediately went looking for other Christians. Someone pointed me to a big husky guy filled with tattoos on his face, sitting at a table. I hoped this was not a trap and this guy really was a Christian brother. Much to my relief, he was and we became good friends. Immediately, I became plugged into the chapel and found out there was going to be a church service in the yard later that evening. I was anxious to attend. That night, my new friend and I stepped onto the yard and I could hear the voices singing songs of praise and worship. My heart felt comforted.

The church at Chuckawalla was completely different from Ironwood. Here, the chapel was open daily, all day long. The inmates ran the Chuckawalla church program. A Christian brother named Jeff was the inmate pastor and Carlos was his assistant. They were both fired up for the Lord and wanted to build up the church. Jeff was the charismatic-styled preacher while Carlos was more of the teacher type.

I started to seek God for what He wanted me to do. In the meantime, I began attending services and held small Bible studies on the yard. Soon, I felt encouraged to take my next step by asking Jeff and Carlos if I could meet with them. In our meeting, I shared my ministry experience and my desire to serve in church in any way they felt I might be a good fit. Jeff and Carlos smiled in unison and received me with the love of God.

The Chuckawalla church had a dedicated group of brothers who wanted to be used by God. We viewed prison as a spiritual boot camp, not a place of confinement. We attended church almost every day. Bible study was from 1:00 pm to 2:00 pm, and prayer from 3:00 pm to 4:00 pm, and we finished off with night service from 6:30 pm to 9:00 pm. We plowed through this spiritual training day after day.

We experienced magnificent manifestations of the power of God in our midst. Frequently, we would march in a circle around the sanctuary, praising and singing to the Lord. Once while we were in the middle of intense worship, an inmate walked in from lifting weights. He shared that he was lifting weights and was overcome by something pulling him to the chapel. He immediately hopped over the fence of the workout area and came over to the church. That evening, that inmate surrendered his life to the Lord. The following day, a pastor from outside of the prison came in to share a sermon. Before he began preaching, the pastor shared a vision he'd had the previous night about our ministry. In his vision, he saw an angel calling a prisoner to the chapel to receive Christ. We were all elated and began to worship God immediately.

Soon though, I would experience one of my biggest trials. One night I was playing cards in the dayroom with a couple Christians. Then a Black Christian came to the table to play too. We were having fun until one of the young Christians got a cup of cold tea.

Prison is very racial and segregated. The different races stick to their own kind. The Blacks have their own side of the dayroom and the Mexicans theirs. Even the showers are segregated. Because of our faith, Christians usually tested the lines of racism. But some Christians have even been stabbed for walking with someone of a different race.

I knew once that cup of tea was brought to the table, all 600 eyes in the day room would be on us. There is a major rule against cross drinking amongst races in prison. My heart started to beat fast, knowing the danger upon us. My worst nightmare came true when the young Christian offered a drink to the Black Christian. He took a drink and then passed the cup to me. Was I going to accept it? I knew it would mark me for a beat down or possible stabbing. My heart was torn.

On one end, I didn't want to deny my faith in Christ by refusing to be associated with my Black Christian brother. But on the other, I didn't want to get beat down. What was I to do? My faith led me to drink of the cup.

Within minutes, a young gang member walked up to the table to call away the young Christian sitting with us. A group of prisoners jumped on him in the corner, busting him up for drinking with an African-American. I couldn't sleep that night. We were in an open dorm and I knew I was next for a beat down. They could get me while I was asleep. Fear was trying to take me down. Finally, I fell asleep quoting the Bible to strengthen my heart.

Two dreaded nights later, I was standing in the dayroom when I looked up at my cubicle. I noticed there was a big guy standing next to my bed. "That guy don't belong there," I thought. Something inside of me told me that he was there for me. A thought flashed through my mind, "I'll stay in the dayroom all night." But then I realized I had to go to sleep some time. I gathered my strength to walk to my bed.

I passed him by and started to open my locker up. "What if he knocks you out? If your locker opens, he'll take all your stuff," I thought quickly. I just played with the lock and then turned around. BOOM! I felt a fist hit my cheekbone. It stunned me and I braced for more.

"This ain't Disneyland. You can't be mingling with the Blacks," the big guy in front of me said.

Something inside of me rose up and I responded, "God bless you man."

He looked just as shocked as me and then walked away.

That was it? I lay on my bed, thinking about what just happened. I knew it wasn't much, but I just got persecuted for my faith in Christ. Wow! That experience made me stronger. But don't get me wrong, I was glad it was over. I could sleep better now.

Back at the chapel, the church was growing. Therefore, Jeff began to organize the church more formally. We held a special service for brothers who were appointed as servants in the church. I was very excited when I was appointed to serve as an elder. I was now able to preach and teach in the church. Then my next test happened.

One day while I was standing in the day room, I saw a couple guys who needed someone to play dominos with, so I joined them. When I introduced myself to my domino partner, I noticed a tattoo on his hand. The tattoo identified him as a gang member from the rival gang my crime was committed against. His name was Clown. My heart started to beat fast, because I knew I was in immediate danger again.

I had never been this close to a rival gang member and I certainly never played on the same team with one. It was too late for me to get up, so I just remained calm and continued to play like nothing was wrong. Soon I realized that he didn't have to know who I was, and I sure wasn't going to volunteer any information. Here was my chance to get to know someone who, if we were on the streets, we would have tried to hurt each other. As strange as it sounds, I always imagined how a rival gang member lived.

After a few days of getting to know Clown, I really started to like him as a friend. He was just like me in many ways. He was tall, funny and cool. Wow, the devil really blinded us back in the days. This was such an eye opener for me. It helped me to realize how foolish I was to commit my crime. I was saddened when Clown eventually got transferred to another prison.

God always has plans that are definitely not our own. Unexpectedly, the assistant pastor, Carlos, was moved to another yard. Our lead pastor, Jeff, was saddened by the move because they had bonded in friendship. We were all hurt by the loss of Carlos. He was an integral member of our revival movement and a powerful Bible teacher. Soon after Pastor Carlos' departure, Jeff called me into the office.

"Hey, Brian, I wanted to let you know that you have really been doing a fantastic job," said Pastor Jeff.

"Thanks, Jeff. I am just so happy to see all of the things God is doing," I added.

"Well, Brian, now that Carlos is gone, we are going to need you to step up."

"Wow, yes! I would love to serve in any way you see fit. I've been praying for God to use me more."

"Brian, I would like to invite you to be the assistant pastor."

I was so stunned and excited by the invitation. I immediately accepted and thanked God for what He had done for me. For me, this was a huge sign of how far I had come in my walk with God.

Prison ministry is intense. We deal with men who have major emotional and character problems. People come off of the streets with narcissistic personalities. These men have developed animosity in their hearts and live in a world of isolation. Our hope is to see the Holy Spirit penetrate those dark and hurting areas that cause men to be destructive towards others and themselves. I believe that without the power of God flowing through our lives, we can never be effective.

During a Bible study about the Holy Spirit, several men were in a circle and we stood up at the end to pray. While we prayed, the power of the Holy Spirit came on everyone strongly. We were all touched by the presence of the Lord. Men began to weep and cry out to God, asking for forgiveness of their sins. For many, this was their first experience of the Holy Spirit's power. The men walked away feeling uplifted and relieved of their inner pain.

After a few months of being the assistant, Jeff called me into the office to hold a meeting. He shared with me that he was going to be transferred soon, and that I should prepare to step up again. This was amazing news for me! God's word over me was being fulfilled more and more. However, Jeff warned me that upon his departure, I could expect the devil to attack me like never before.

"New levels bring new devils," he warned.

Perhaps I did not take Jeff's warning as seriously as I should have, but I went away to pray in a corner. Jeff shared with me that he was concerned how the elder board would receive me as the inmate pastor. I was only twenty-two, and the rest of the elders ranged in ages from thirty to forty. Finally, Jeff called a meeting to share with them about his transfer and about me. At the meeting, no one was openly opposed to me becoming the new leader. But I sensed an undercurrent feeling of jealously.

After Jeff left, I called another elders' meeting. I shared with them my outlook on ministry and passionate desire to impact the prison for Jesus. It was then reconfirmed that I would lead and a brother named Chris would become my assistant. Chris was a tall, humble man in his early forties. He had been in prison for almost twenty years and he was extremely knowledgeable in the Word. He was a gifted teacher of the Bible and a great help to me. He gave my youthful face a sense of legitimacy in the eyes of others.

Immediately, I began preparing to preach every Sunday night. On the second Sunday, God filled the chapel. The usher at the door was stunned to see all of the men wanting to enter. We knew God was answering our prayers. We had a powerful time in the Lord that night. The ministry really began to blossom. Many young brothers were eager to serve in the church. Many nights after returning to my bunk, I would sit in awe of God and how far He had brought me from the barrio.

Our chaplain at Chuckwalla was Reverend Dean Parker. Chaplain Parker was new and still becoming familiar with each of the churches on the various yards within the prison. He was a tall and slender elderly man, a Baptist preacher. He felt the Lord had blessed him to become the new chaplain. A chaplain's job is hard work and Chaplain Parker showed genuine concern for us, as he wanted to help us overcome our pasts. He began holding meetings with us to assess our ministry goals and needs.

Soon I would become the target of a vicious spiritual attack. This time, not from the world, but from within the church. Two elders in the church were conspiring to have me removed as the pastor. My youthful zeal for the Lord rubbed them the wrong way. They started falsely accusing me of racism and favoritism. Chaplain Parker convened a special meeting in the chapel with the church and leaders.

It felt like I was on trial. The church elders were the witnesses and the jury. They sat up on the platform and charged me with everything they could think of. I knew I wasn't that bad. What had happened? I just wanted to serve the Lord. Finally, Chaplain Parker stood up.

"I'm saddened to subject Brian to all these accusations. And I probably shouldn't have had this type of meeting. But because of the accusations, I'm going to sit down Brian from position of pastor for a period of time."

This was a blow to my spirit. How could this happen? Christians are not supposed to be like this. Christians are supposed to be loving and kind. I began to wrestle with thoughts of anger and bitterness. It ate me up inside that those jealous elders got their way. But what could I do? I decided to resign from chapel ministry.

I moped around in discouragement for a couple weeks. I couldn't understand what was happening. I reminded myself of the word I received from the Lord a few years back. My faith began to rise again. I knew God had a plan for me. I had to persevere to the end.

Meanwhile, I had the idea to begin a newsletter called "World for Jesus." I thought perhaps I could reach more people through God stories in people's lives. I shared my vision with one of my friends and we began to draw a rough draft. We went to the library to get addresses of different churches. We began to draw greeting cards that we could sell to other inmates to pay for the stamps we needed.

This was a labor of love for us. Our desire to reach out to the world with the Gospel was driving us. We had appealing testimonies and knew that our personal backgrounds would draw people to read it. Soon we decided to throw a rally on the yard to promote our "World for Jesus" magazine. We knew this would ignite controversy in the church because it wasn't a chapel-sanctioned event. We went forward anyway. We made flyers and passed them out to inmates on the yard. Late that evening, we put two bleachers together by faith and announced over an intercom for prisoners to come out to celebrate with us. The rally was successful, but we had much to learn.

The years were going by and I remained prayerful and passionate about being released one day. However, I tried to focus on my present journey and the work God was having me do within the prison system. I wanted to go home, but I knew I had work to do here too.

Back at the chapel, Chaplain Parker decided to reorganize the ministry and invited me back. I agreed, even though I was no longer the pastor. We agreed on bylaws that allowed a voting system that created equality among the elders. The new ministry was set up like a triangle, in which newcomers could come in and start off as an usher. It was a new beginning for us in the ministry and things started really moving forward.

One day while I was sitting on the ground in front of the chapel, my friend, Greg brought up the idea of me speaking to the prison's Re-Entry Class. Re-Entry is a program that most inmates go through prior to being released from prison. The graduation was in two days, and we did not know how or even if I could get cleared to go. Finally, a friend of ours had an opportunity to approach the Re-Entry teacher and suggest to her that I might have a positive effect on her class. To my delight, the teacher decided to let me try it out. I was so excited to get my pass, it read "Re-Entry Graduation," and if you took it on face value, it read as if I was graduating from Re-Entry Class. I held onto that moment and accepted by faith that this was another sign from God that I would be released from prison one day.

I had one night to prepare my notes, so I stayed up late in the day-room, thinking about what I was going to say. It was going to be a great opportunity for me to share my story to prisoners who would never go to the chapel. I woke up early the next morning and got all dressed up with shiny shoes and my creased state-issued pants. Finally, a guard came to escort me to the Re-Entry graduation. I walked with my head held high as if it were my own graduation day. The classroom was filled with prisoners looking hard core, and to my surprise the teacher sat me with the prison officials. My heart started to race. I was seated with the associate warden, the head of education, a captain, a sergeant, and other officials. I silently thanked God as my thoughts trailed off to the Bible verse that reads, "A man's gift maketh room for him, and brings him before great men" (Proverbs 18: 16, KJV).

The time was getting closer for me to speak. Looking across the room, I could tell many of the inmates wondered who I was, why was I there, and how had I received clearance to sit among the prison officials. I was wondering the same thing myself. After some time, the teacher introduced me and I walked up behind the podium.

"I am thankful to the prison officials for allowing me to speak today, and I give honor to my Savior Jesus Christ for who I am today."

There was not an expectation for this to be a religious speech, however, I knew God had given me an opportunity to encourage these men. I continued in my talk to urge the men to value their freedom. I challenged them to step up and take their positions as fathers, leaders, and mentors of the next generation. I shared with the men that I was the youngest inmate on B-Yard with a life sentence, and at the age of sixteen I had thrown my life away. I looked out into the crowd and watched faces turn from shock to compassion. I am sure my story made those men think of their own lives, troubles, and now potential for eternal freedom. After I finished speaking, the teacher assured me that my story was what her class needed to hear. Additionally, the associate warden approved me to speak at every Re-Entry class graduation throughout the prison. Wow!

I worked hard to remain committed to my spiritual growth. The years were going by and things seemed to be going really well in my life and within my church work. God had used me to help many others. I had almost completely blocked out of my mind my friend Jeff's warning, that the more I became involved in ministry, the more I would open myself up for spiritual attacks. And Jeff was right. Years after Jeff was gone and things were at a high with the ministry, the devil began to strategically launch some of the biggest fiery darts he ever sent my way. The devil's darts left me shaken, with nowhere to turn.

Brian & Laura's

wedding, Chuckawalla Prison

Brian preaching

at Chuckawalla Prison

## CHAPTER 9

# A PINE BOX

According to the State of California, "Only inmates sentenced to life in prison, with the possibility of parole, are subject to suitability hearings by BPH [Board of Parole Hearing]. It is not uncommon for inmates to receive many parole hearings before they are found suitable for release." On paper, the laws that govern parole and a parole hearing sound like a simple process free of technicality and emotion. On the other hand, having to undergo the parole hearing process is like riding a roller coaster track backwards, handcuffed and blindfolded, pedaling on a unicycle. I found I was left unsure if I would ever make it out.

Since I was in prison, I met many lifer prisoners who had been in prison for over twenty years. Many of them were mad at the world and disgruntled about life. They would often make it a point to tell me, "Brian, you're never going to go home. You're going to die in prison like us." I would face this negativity every day. Some of the older lifers would even mock me at times, "Here comes Brian. He thinks he's going home."

A lot of the older lifers' anger and bitterness came from the bro-kenness of the prison system. The past governor, Pete Wilson, had an unofficial "no parole" policy with lifer prisoners. And now the current governor, Gray Davis, vowed that no lifer would be released on his watch except in a pine box. A friend had sent me a letter with a newspaper clipping inside. The headline read, "[Governor] Davis rarely approves the release of convicted killers." In his term as governor, Gray Davis had the ability to parole 267 inmates with murder sentences, but only approved the release of eight. Governor Davis' unjustified denials were like crushing roundhouse kicks to lifer prisoners.

Late 2001, amidst all of the church ministry success, I was notified that I was scheduled to have my first parole hearing in a few months. I was through the roof with guarded excitement. I had been warned by many old time lifers never to get excited about a parole hearing because the outcome would not be good. My lawyer told me only 0.5 percent of all people who go before the parole board get found suitable for parole, and this is after years of being in prison. Everyone was pessimistic, except me. I spoke with Laura on the phone and we completely ignored all of the naysayers. We both took our prayer to a deeper level of devotion, thanking God for all He had done and believing in His mighty power to allow the parole board to find me suitable for parole. We were asking for nothing less than a miracle.

I went before the parole board in March 2002. I was just twenty-six years old and had only served nine years of a life sentence for a gang-related murder. I had heard horror stories about the intensity of parole hearings. Many hard core prisoners refused to even attend their hearings because they didn't want to be exposed to the verbal attacks by the parole commissioners. Not me. I was scared, but ready to go through whatever it took to get me home.

A guard escorted me into the meeting room and handcuffed me to a chair. In front of me were two parole commissioners, and to the right was a Deputy District Attorney from Los Angeles sent to oppose my release. Man, the parole commissioners looked stern, with no emotions. The atmosphere weighed heavy with pressure. I began to sweat even though the air conditioner was blowing hard. It really felt like I was in the movie *The Matrix* again, about ready to fight for my life.

Finally, the commissioner spoke. She went through a series of reports about my whole life. Then she went off.

"Is it true that your oldest brother was killed in a gang-related shooting?"

"Yes," I whispered.

"Is it true that your second oldest brother was shot in a gang-related shooting?"

"Yes, ma'am."

"Is it also true that you were shot in a gang-related shooting?"

Now I was wondering where she was going with her questions.

"Yes, ma'am."

"Well then, is it true that you knew what you were doing when you committed your crime?"

Wow. This was it. The moment of truth. Many lifers before me have come to this point, just to deny their responsibility for their crime. What was I going to say?

"Regretfully, yes. But I'm sorry for what I have done and take full responsibility for my crime."

The commissioner looked stunned, as if she never heard a lifer prisoner accept responsibility for his or her crime. After the other commissioner reviewed my prison record, the panel turned to the Deputy District Attorney.

"I want to note that I have never seen a prisoner come so prepared to a parole hearing as Mr. Warth has demonstrated here today," he said, to my surprise. Wow! For a second, it seemed like he was going to support me. I was wrong.

"But Mr. Warth has only served nine years of his life sentence and let's not forget he is in prison for a gang-related murder. On behalf of Los Angeles County, I oppose parole for Mr. Warth."

The commissioner then turned to me. "It is now your time to speak out on why you believe you're suitable for parole."

I had waited years for this moment. It seemed like all my public talks prepared me for this one speech. My heart was beating in overdrive. I was getting ready to plead for my life to another human being, and started to shake inside. Then God gave me the strength to speak. After expressing my remorse for my crime and that I was no longer a sixteen-year-old gang member but now a young man with morals and values, I pleaded, "Please have mercy on me by giving me a second chance in life."

I did it.

The commissioner informed me that we were breaking for a recess while they made their decision. The guard came to escort me to a small cell. As soon as the cuffs were off, I fell to my knees, thanking God for a miracle. About twenty minutes later, I was called back into the parole board room.

"Mr. Warth, after reviewing your record today and hearing you out, we have decided that you are now suitable for parole."

Before she even finished pronouncing the word "suitable," my forehead hit the table as tears of relief began to fall from my eyes. Could I be hearing her correctly? Did she say suitable? It felt like a thousand-pound weight was being lifted off my shoulders. A nudge from my lawyer got me to sit upright again.

The prison community was jolted by this miracle. I was the youngest lifer to be found suitable for parole in recent history. People were shocked. Some praised the decision while others glared from a distance in rage and envy. After my parole hearing, I rushed to call my wife.

"Collect call from Chuckawalla Valley State Correctional Facility. Do you accept the charges?" the operator said.

"Yes, I accept," said Laura. "Brian?"

"AAHHHHHHHHHHHH!!!" I screamed into the phone.

"AAAAAHHHHHHHHH!!!" Laura shouted back.

"I was found suitable! I was found suitable!"

"Oh my gosh, babe! I knew it! God is so good! You're going to get to come home."

Laura sounded like she was crying and laughing.

"I don't know all the details yet. But God is so good. My first parole hearing and I was found suitable. It's nobody but Jesus!" I shouted.

Our conversation flowed like a clumsy dance of words. Neither of us took much of a break while both of us stumbled over one another to speak words of love, and joy. Finally we came down off of the initial high. Negative thoughts began to flood my mind.

"What if the governor reverses the decision?"

"Brian, what are you talking about? Why would he do that?"

"I don't know. I was told that the governor has 150 days to review my case and within that time he can reverse the decision," I answered.

Laura and I continued to pray about everything, and as the months went by, no news was good news. On August 16, 2002, I received a parole release review from the governor's office.

"The 1997 psychological evaluation concluded only that his [Mr. Warth's] potential for violence is less now than when he was admitted to prison. Given the level of violence demonstrated in Mr. Warth's crime, this still leaves him an unreasonable risk to public safety. After considering all of the factors, I conclude that Mr. Warth is unsuitable for parole at this time. Accordingly, I reverse the Board's decision," wrote Governor Gray Davis.

I sat in my cell and combed through the release review documents. I thought I was prepared for a denial. In the back of my mind, I always told myself a denial was possible, but seeing it on paper was crushing. This was the kind of news that you would want to receive with your wife sitting lovingly beside you. Even having my dad near would have been great. But I was alone on my bunk, thinking of how I planned to tell Laura that we would not be starting a family any time soon.

The disappointment of my denial weighed heavy on my heart. I felt very cold and lonely. My thoughts drifted to my family and all of the tragedy that had happened to us over the years. I recalled being a little boy at David's funeral. I could remember all of my siblings crying and grieving over our brother's death for weeks, hoping somehow he would return to our family. I had been in prison for over a decade, and none of my siblings visited me or showed any type of concern for me. I rarely received a letter. The devil was trying to use the parole denial to harden my heart toward my family, to feel sorry for myself, and to work against all of the growth that God had invested in me. I could let the sadness mature into anger and return to the old Brian. Nonetheless, I knew that God had created my life with purpose. I recalled all of the Bible's verses that gave me comfort. I dropped to my knees and read the Psalms and asked the Holy Spirit for comfort.

Eventually, I picked myself up out of the heavy fog of disappointment. I thanked God for the opportunity to even be recognized for the possibility of parole. I thought of Jeff's comment, and realized I could not let this setback keep me down. God had a plan for my life and I would keep pushing forward.

However, I did spend time combing through my review. I had made so many changes in my life since committing the crime ten years before. I had grown in so many ways. It was difficult reading on paper that I had once been this empty, cruel, and broken young man. The judgments on these forms followed me because of those few years of foolishness, trying to be cool in gangs. Reflecting on my sentence led me to think how senselessly David lost his life, and how another teenager sat in prison for killing him. How dumb was I to repeat this vicious cycle and pay for it with my life? I hoped now, even more than ever, to encourage gang members in prison to make changes. To become mentors to others so the violence would stop. I was not naïve to think we could influence every gang member in the world, but we could definitely make a good dent with all of the inmates in here.

I moved on from the reversal in 2002. I knew God had other plans. However, year after year I continued to encounter the same opposition with the governor. I was found suitable for parole again in 2003. On August 13, 2003, I received a second letter from Governor Gray Davis, reversing the parole board's decision.

I wondered why he had to type REVERSE in capital letters. Seeing the word reverse capitalized felt personal and final. Once again, I sat on my bunk, combing through the documents, wondering why, if the parole board found me suitable, the governor felt that I was unsuitable. It was like they were playing ping pong with my life.

The fact that I was found suitable again really empowered my family and me to keep our hopes high. I knew God had a plan and I tried to remain upbeat. Laura and I continued to pray, believing that something big was ahead. I constantly fought off doubt and fear. If prison was where He wanted me, then this was where I would stay, but I still believed with all my heart that I would be released one day. I just had to be patient and wait on God's timing and favor.

Soon God would shake California for me.

Brian's ordination

ceremony, Chuckawalla Prison

## CHAPTER 10

# THE GOVERNATOR

═══════════════════════════════

I n 2003, a political typhoon began to form against Governor Davis, who came under fire for a major electricity crisis. Thousands of people were affected by rolling blackouts, even us out there in the desert. We would go days with no electricity in the scorching hot desert heat. It was horrible, almost unbearable. Many prisoners would fall out under heat exhaustion.

Then the governor came under attack for a major budget deficit. I guess you don't mess with people's money, because this crisis initiated a historic governor recall election. This was huge, the first gubernatorial recall in California history. Wow! My radical faith entertained the thought that maybe God was removing the governor just for me.

Because of the rules of the recall election, it was easy for just about anyone to get qualified to run for the office of governor. You had all kinds of crazy people running for governor, including many celebrities like Gary Coleman from *Diff'rent Strokes* and the mega star, Arnold Schwarzenegger from *The Terminator*.

Soon Arnold Schwarzenegger became the forerunner in the pack. I immediately started to research Arnold's views on politics. Arnold was a self-made millionaire who spent years on Venice Beach, body building. Some of the old-time prisoners would tell me stories about how Arnold used to smoke weed and party all the time. I figured someone with that background might be more lenient on lifers.

And then it happened.

Gray Davis was kicked out of office and Arnold Schwarzenegger was swept into power. I remember the television being on in the day room and there were cheers from the prisoners when Schwarzenegger won. The change in power meant a possible new start for many lifers, including me. Soon the media dubbed Arnold "The Governator."

About a month later, a newspaper article pinned to the wall in the dayroom caught my attention. I walked over to get a closer look at the headline. To my surprise it read, "Governor Will Not Block Parole Board." I quickly read it, as my heart started to race. It reported that Governor Schwarzenegger said he would allow the parole board to do their job, thus allowing their parole decisions to stand.

Tears started to fall down my face. God was up to something major in my life.

I continued ministering at the chapel and hosting large World for Jesus Rallies on the yard. We would convert the prison gym into the Chuckawalla Dome. Our version of the Staple Center in Los Angeles. One time we had half the prison yard population at our event. God was using my life to impact hundreds and hundreds of prisoners.

One major highlight of my prison experience was the day of my Ordination Ceremony. Very few prisoners have ever been ordained while they were still incarcerated. I was blessed to have chaplains to sponsor me and believe I was fit to be set a part for the work of the Lord.

Chaplain Banks had been my mentor since my CYA days. He had moved on to be a chaplain in the Arkansas Department of Corrections. But flew in the previous night for this special occasion.

Chaplain George McDonald served as the Executive Director of prison ministries for Western Baptist State Convention of the National Baptist Convention, USA, Inc., the nation's oldest and largest African American religious convention.

They each carried a clerical robe draped over their right arms. They also had an extra robe, which was black with two golden crosses embroidered on the front. It was for me, for they had come on a mission to ordain me as a licensed minister of the Gospel of the Lord Jesus Christ.

They greeted one another with a hug and briefly talked about past times. I had not seen Chaplain Banks for like ten years, making this moment feel so surreal.

Then the chaplains led me into a private room wherein they held a formal Examining Council session. Chaplain McDonald led the inquiry.

"Who called you to the ministry?" he asked.

"The Lord Jesus did, when He touched my heart over ten years ago," I answered.

To my surprise, the chaplains didn't make grand proclamations about the future success of my ministry. Instead, they admonished me to remain humble and to forgive those who would offend me.

I wrote in my journal, "The overriding principles that were impressed upon my heart were, 'forgive those who offend you, take your suffering as Jesus did, and preach in season and out of season.'"

Chaplain Banks capped everything with, "Your first ministry is to your wife and family."

After many other questions were answered and we read the Bible together, the call was confirmed – the Ordination Ceremony would continue.

The chapel was beautifully decorated with two large banners. One declared, *Confirming the Call*, and the other, *The Missionary Journey*.

*The Missionary Journey* was decorated with pictures of my life. The earliest picture was of me at seven years old, playing baseball, and one of the latest was taken of me preaching the Gospel in the Chuckawalla Dome. My parents were also pictured, but the one that stood out was taken with my wife, Laura. By God's grace, she had stuck by my side through my entire journey.

Within minutes of the yard opening, the chapel was jam-packed. All nationalities, all shapes and complexions filled the seats. Many were even standing. One guest expressed his amazement that so many inmates came out to give me their support.

I walked into the sanctuary and sat on one of the chairs lined up on the platform. Next to me on a wooden jacket hanger hung the extra black robe.

Chaplains Banks and McDonald, now both wearing their clerical robes, walked down the aisle with Chaplain Parker. They knelt down on their knees and prayed before sitting.

The atmosphere was filled with a heavy sense of reverence. The prisoners there had never attended such a ceremony.

Chaplain Banks began to speak, "Throughout history, God has called workers to carry out His will. Righteous Noah was chosen to survive the flood and save his family through building the ark. Abraham, the man of faith, was selected to be the forerunner of God's holy nation, Israel. Jesus chose the Twelve to be His apostles.

The early church set apart those called to special work through prayer and the laying on of hands."

"We come today to formally ordain our brother, Brian Warth, to the work for which God has called him. We seek to honor only Christ, and this one is being set apart for just that purpose. Let us invoke God's blessing upon this occasion."

Chaplain McDonald then stood behind the pulpit. He asked Chaplain Parker and Chaplain Banks to escort me to the altar.

I stood between both elder saints, giants in the faith in my eyes. Men who gave their lives for the outcasts of society.

"God has His hand on you, Brian," Chaplain McDonald said, as he declared the spiritual charge and anointed me with oil.

"Do you believe the Old and New Testament are the Word of God?"

"I do," I answered.

"Do you solemnly commit to be a worker and servant of God, rightly dividing the Word of God?

"I do."

Chaplain McDonald instructed Chaplain Parker and Chaplain Banks to clothe me with the black robe.

He continued, "In the Name of the Lord Jesus Christ you are hereby ordained to preach God's word. We send you in the Name of Jesus Christ and may Christ anoint you and the Holy Spirit empower you."

Wow, for a moment in time, I felt free from the craziness of prison life.

But it wasn't long before I was slapped in the face with the cold realities of prison again. For as many prisoners who were turning to the Lord, violence still ensued between the races, gangs and rivalries. I was housed in a dorm that was built for 150 people but now housed 350. If you pried the top of the building off, we would look like a can of sardines. Desert heat would soar upwards of 120 degrees. We had no air conditioning. Swamp Coolers ran throughout the day, but only took the temperature down maybe just a few degrees. My bunk was along a cement wall, which the sun beamed on all day long. No matter where a bunk was located, a prisoner had other inmates above, adjacent, below and all around. There was no beating the heat or the lack of privacy at Chuckawalla.

One night I was ready for my shower. Each tier had its own set of showers. The bottom tier had shower stalls that could hold up to sixteen people at one time. I headed to shower and I saw two Hispanic guys, one tall and the other short and husky, who reminded me of a bulldog. The two men were arguing extremely loudly in Spanish as they showered. I recognized the bulldog guy from the yard. Every day at three o'clock in the afternoon, at the height of the desert heat, the bulldog guy would work out with the punching bag. Punch, punch, punch, punch, punch! No matter how hot it was or how many times he punched the bag, it would appear he would never tire. I knew he had a life sentence.

I wondered what the two guys were arguing about, but I had absolutely no intentions of getting involved. In prison we had strict rules. The only people who stopped fights were guards. Unless you cared to possibly lose your life.

Suddenly, the arguing abruptly stopped. The bulldog guy told the tall guy to meet him outside after the shower. He ended the conversation as quickly as it started. I was taking my shower in the middle of this heated conversation. I was keeping to myself as much as possible. However, when the bulldog guy said, "That's it. Conversation over. Meet me outside," I got the feeling I needed to hurry up and remove myself from this scene. I made it through years of prison because I learned how to avoid altercations.

I hurried to finish my shower and went back to my cubicle area. I dressed and decided to head outside to pick up my photos that a few of my fellow inmates had taken. Just as I was walking out, I heard the siren alarms begin to sound. Next, come the forceful sounds of guards: "Get down! Get down! Everyone down!" This was not a request? No matter where you were on the grounds, even if you were on the cement and it was baking at 130 degrees, you had to immediately go face down on the ground. I hit the floor, and I saw the correction officers running towards my building. A few minutes later, I saw the bulldog guy being escorted out in handcuffs. Guards were spraying water on his face because he clearly had been sprayed with mace. Moments after that, I saw a body being carried out on what inmates called the orange canoe. It was a gurney, but shaped and painted just like a canoe. Use of the canoe meant a person was seriously injured, if not dead.

Finally, we heard the signal for a yard recall, which meant each inmate must return to his bunk. As I walked back to my bunk, I saw giant puddles of blood everywhere. It looked like an animal slaughterhouse. The blood was pooled even near my bunk. Flies began circle around the puddles. A prison guard came dressed in a HAZMAT suit to begin the sterilization process.

As I sat on my bunk and stared at the blood that covered the floors and walls, I began to think how badly I wanted to go home and leave this hell hole. I had a personal crisis and reality check, and I yearned to be away from the insanity of prison. I wanted to be with my wife and family. I did not want to live like this forever.

With a life sentence, it is dangerous to begin missing the outside world. I could drive myself crazy thinking about something I had no control over.

In 2005, I was up for my third parole hearing. After all of the recent violence, I prayed hard that I would be found suitable to go home again. With a new governor in office, I thought surely if I were found suitable, the governor would not block my release. This process was not just taxing on me, but more so on my wife and dad, both financially and emotionally. It cost almost $5,000 per hearing for lawyer fees, and way more than that for any appeals filed.

Once again, in 2005 the parole board found me suitable for parole. I was so excited! I waited anxiously for the governor's response. People were already telling me goodbye. But then five months later, I received the following disappointing letter from Governor Arnold Schwarzenegger, "Mr. Warth now age 29, has demonstrated increased maturity, self-control, and good behavior in prison – and he is absolutely on the right track for parole. But after serving less than 13 years of his 16-to-life sentence, I cannot conclude at this time, given the current record before me and after carefully considering the very same factors the Board must consider, that he is suitable for parole because the gravity of the murder he committed presently outweighs the positive factors supporting his parole. Accordingly, because I believe his release from prison would pose an unreasonable risk of danger to society, I REVERSE the Board's 2004 decision to grant parole to Mr. Warth." Signed Arnold Schwarzenegger.

What a bummer. This was a terrible process. A rigged process. A sham. How could all three of the parole board's decisions be wrong? Governor Schwarzenegger reneged on his promise and caved in to political pressure. And so went the horrible process two more times. By 2007, I was probably the only lifer prisoner to have received five consecutive parole grants by the parole board and five reversals by the governor. I was never denied parole by the parole board.

My last parole reversal really knocked me down, spiritually and emotionally. I thought for sure I would be going home. I was confident God was going to answer my prayer, but He didn't. It was the first time I was ever really crushed since I started walking with God. I was used to God spoiling me, and now it felt like He was a million miles away.

I walked around the prison yard, confused. I laid on my bunk, staring at the cement wall as I cried. I kneeled down in the chapel and cried some more. I started to doubt if it was God's will for me to go home. I wanted so bad to be mad at God. I wanted to scream at Him. But honestly, I was too afraid of God to be mad at Him because I didn't even deserve to live. Deep down inside, I knew it was only because of God's mercy I was still alive.

A song by Ginny Owens, which I never heard before, began to minister to my heart:

*The pathway is broken and the signs are unclear.*
*And I don't know the reasons why you brought me here.*
*But just because You love me the way that You do.*
*I'm gonna walk through the valley if you want me to.*
[If You Want Me To, Without Condition, 1999]

The lyrics awakened my soul. I had to make up my mind. It was time to lay down my dreams, time to abandon my aspirations at the foot of the cross. I shared my heart with my wife, and eventually, I let go of holding on to going home.

"God, it doesn't matter to me anymore if I go home or die in this prison. I will continue to serve You no matter where I'm at."

This was more a prayer of commitment than anything. Like the three Hebrews in the Book of Daniel, who were threatened by fire, yet told the king even if God didn't deliver them they would still not bow down. After my prayer, I felt a sense of peace as I left things in God's hands. I would have to live each day as is and simply be the best man God made me to be.

After moving on from that rejection in 2007, I had a new perspective on life. However, this did not mean I gave up the fight for my release and restoration. It actually gave Laura and me a surge of faith. Unknown to me, Laura had been battling the shame and fear of letting people know about my incarceration. Through the years, she had developed into a pillar in the community, building relationships with the mayor, city council and business people.

She tried her best to keep my situation a secret. She feared people would shun her for what I did. Plus, her Realty business could be affected if the community no longer viewed her in a positive light. But God began to deal with her about her fear. Could it be possible that God empowered her to develop so many influential relationships to eventually help aid my release?

Laura came to the end of herself. She decided to cast off her fear and approach people for help with securing my release. Over the next year, she worked feverishly at preparing for my next parole hearing. She started the Free Brian Campaign, which had a website to raise support from the local community. Laura gathered a team of friends, family, and colleagues and knocked on doors, met with the mayor, vice mayor, and city council members. She began explaining our situation and asking for support letters. Before I knew it, she had racked up major support from all over our local community.

One day, I called Laura and found out she had managed through business relationships to get a meeting with Sheriff Lee Baca of Los

Angeles County. Laura, accompanied by a city official and police captain, was escorted in a patrol car to Sheriff Baca's office. With limited time available, Laura began to plead my case to Sheriff Baca. Part of the governor's decision on granting parole is based upon letters he receives from the sheriff's office. In the past, the sheriff's office had sent letters opposing my release. Sheriff Baca shared that in a case like mine, he believed I should not have a second chance. Laura shared that she maintained her grace and decided to move on to the next person.

Instead of feeling down about the situation, Laura felt that if she could end up in a private meeting with Sheriff Lee Baca, then God definitely had His hand in this situation. Laura would not give up. She continued to collect letters of support from hundreds of people. The Free Brian Campaign was in full force. If you lived in or near our community, you probably had heard of Laura and me. One day during a phone call, Laura shared with me that after a visit with a well-known English teacher in the area, the teacher encouraged Laura to head to a book signing that Maria Shriver was participating in near Los Angeles. Maria Shriver was the governor's wife.

Laura grabbed her mom and her niece and headed down to the book signing. Without a plan, Laura and my mother-in-law formed a line to have Maria Shriver sign their books. Amazingly, Laura and her mom made it to the end of the line in the knick of time. Laura, my mother-in-law, and my niece were the last three people in line. Eventually, the ladies came up with the keen idea to give Ms. Shriver a "Free Brian Campaign" letter, which stated my situation and listed all of my accomplishments. On that campaign letter, my mother-in-law wrote a note that said, "Please read: from one mother to another."

We will never know if it was the note passed across a book signing table to the governor's wife, if Sheriff Lee Baca had changed his mind, or maybe the hundreds of support letters that jammed the governor's fax machine. But something definitely changed in 2008.

I had my sixth parole hearing on a Thursday in 2008. I walked in with guarded hope. The parole board found me suitable for parole again. I left the hearing vowing to not be anxious. I would be waiting for several months before knowing the verdict. There is always that glimmer of hope that this would be the time.

Living in the desert was like being in a sauna all day long. I was standing in the sun, waiting to go to the prison store. The five-month parole review process on my last parole date had just passed a day before. I could not help but think my release was blocked again, although I had not received any official notice. The whole process was a constant battle between my faith and doubts.

As I stood waiting in line, the lady in charge of the store approached me.

"Hey Brian, has the governor approved your parole date yet?"

"I haven't heard anything yet. But I think he blocked my release again."

"When you go home, make sure you don't mess up."

I was shocked by her response. Did she misunderstand me? Her response left me confused. I tried to shake it off, but that only led me to thinking about adjusting to another year in this hellhole.

I bought my store goods and headed to my bunk. I lay there, just staring at the gray concrete wall. Man, this prison thing was rough. How was I going to tell Laura I wasn't going home again? I picked up my Bible to read whatever I could find.

The page flipped to Hebrews 6:10-12, "For God is not unjust to forget your work and labor of love which you have shown toward

His name, in that you have ministered to the saints, and do minister. And we desire that each of you show the same diligence to the full assurance of hope to the end, that you do not become sluggish, but imitate those who through faith and patience inherit the promises." Wow! Was God speaking to me again?

About an hour later, a blood gang member named Low Down walked up to my bunk.

"Can I talk to you?" he asked.

Thinking maybe he wanted counseling, I said to myself that I was not in the mood to help anyone while I was hurting.

"I need to talk to you, dog," he persisted.

He then sat on my bunk. This surprised me, because it was against prison rules to sit on a bunk of a different ethnicity.

"What's happening," I said.

"Can you keep a secret?"

I thought maybe one of his family members died.

"Yeah, I can."

"No, dog. Can you really keep a secret? What I'm about to tell you, you can't even tell your wife."

I sat up, showing my intense interest in what he was about to say.

"Tell me what's up!"

"Did you hear what the lady in charge of the store told you?"

"Yeah, why?"

"Dog, she couldn't tell you straight up. But she wanted to tell you the governor approved your release. You're going home next week."

"Are you serious?" I said with shock. "Don't mess with me, man!"

"Dog, you're going home!"

Suddenly, this strange feeling came over my body. It was the chills. The hairs on my arms stood up. My eyes began to well up with water. Could this be it? Was my dream finally coming true?

I wanted to tell Laura so badly. But I gave my word and had to keep it. I ran downstairs to call her anyway.

She had already vowed not to come to the prison anymore. It was her way of taking a stand of faith, trusting God to release me.

"Why don't you come visit me this Sunday?" I asked.

"I already told you I wasn't going up there anymore."

Laura noticed the change in the tone of my voice. It was more upbeat now. Of course it was. I was hiding the biggest secret of my life. She changed her mind about coming up, which made me happier.

On Saturday, Laura came to visit. She commented that my demeanor was different. Nonetheless, I still could not tell her what I knew about coming home. Laura commented that she had a confirmed feeling from the Lord that I was coming home, and this was her last visit to Chuckawalla. I didn't tell her my secret. Instead, I acted like I really believed God was going to release me. I was Mr. Faith guy again

When Monday morning came around, I was anxious to find out the official news. I wanted to run to the program office where all the case managers were. I did not run, but I surely did walk fast. I stood close by the door, waiting for a case manager to stick his or her head out. Finally one did.

"Excuse me, sir. I'm a lifer and I have been waiting to hear from the governor on my parole date. Can you check for me?"

Five minutes and a million heartbeats later, the case manager came back out with a piece of paper in his hands. This was the moment of truth.

"Congratulations, Brian, you're going home in the morning."

"Wow! It's official."

The case manager smiled and shook my hand.

Word spread fast throughout the prison yard. Everyone was congratulating me. Gang members, drug addicts, and officers alike all wished me well with a flurry of congratulations.

My last night in prison was a killer. I could not sleep. So many thoughts bombarded my mind. Exhausted from excitement, I nodded off to sleep for a few hours. Finally, I sat up, filled with joy, knowing this was not an ordinary day at Chuckawalla. Today was the day God would answer our prayers.

I grabbed my stuff to walk out of the door for the last time.

My dear friend, Leo walked along with me. He was older than me and still had ten years to do on his prison sentence. We grew close in prison, formed a bond like two soldiers in the trenches of war. He walked me all the way to the gate. We prayed and I continued to walk.

I can still recall him standing there watching me as I faded away into the distance.

I was put in one last holding cell to await my release. Because of my prison sentence, I had to be escorted home by two armed parole officers. My heart was beating fast. I sat in the front seat of a car for the first time in sixteen years without chains and handcuffs. As we drove, butterflies flew wildly in my stomach. I stared deeply into the prison one last time. My perspective was different from the outside. I noticed the high gates, spiny barbed wire, and impenetrable concrete walls. Each line of the building's architecture was filled with memories. I had grown up here in this impassable jungle, surviving its dangers within. This concrete fortress was supposed to be my graveyard. A place I was sent, never to return or be heard from again.

Instead, by God's grace, I rise!

Brian & Laura at Brian's welcome

home party at church

Brian & mother

on day of his release

Brian sharing his story at

a Los Angeles High School

# EPILOGUE

I t has been twenty-one years since I was first arrested. My life has been a long, winding journey. I was born in Los Angeles, turned sixteen in Texas, seventeen in a L.A. Juvenile Hall, eighteen in the L.A. County Jail, nineteen and twenty in the California Youth Authority, twenty-one in Chino State Prison, twenty-two in Ironwood State Prison and and went from age twenty-three to thirty-two in Chuckawalla Valley State Prison, when I was released. Only by God's grace have I come this far. Many of the teenagers who were arrested near the same time as me are still in maximum-security prisons, with no hope for release.

I know how it feels to have no hope, to watch as your future is shattered. I know how it feels to throw away your life and experience the pain of hurting others and hurting your family. But I also know what it feels like to not give up, and to struggle back to where you're supposed to be in life. I am no longer hopeless, but have discovered why I'm still alive.

I am deeply sorry for the hurt I have caused. The regret for my mistakes fuels me to help other youth to make the right decisions. Just like the Apostle Paul's drive to build up the Church came through his understanding that he once tried to destroy it.

God has done so much for me. The Lord took me in when the world kicked me out. He loved, protected, and transformed me. God put me back on the right track and gave me a vision to impact the world for good. Now I am forever indebted to His cause — the cause of the Gospel!

*Brian Warth resides in Greater Long Beach, California, with his lovely family and is the founder and Lead Pastor of Chapel of Change Christian Fellowship, a fast-growing, multi-ethnic, city-focused, river church dedicated to giving fresh hope to families and the city. He is available to share his powerful story at your church or event. You can learn more about his church and speaking ministry at www.chapelofchange.org.*

Chapel of Change Christian Fellowship
P.O. Box 1844
Paramount, CA 90723